IN

THE

BEGIN

NING

Illustrated Stories from the Old Testament

Serge Bloch
Frédéric Boyer

Translated by Cole Swensen

CHRONICLE BOOKS
SAN FRANCISCO

Long ago, going back more than 2,600 years, Jehoiakim was king of Judah and based in Jerusalem. He succeeded legendary kings who had resisted a succession of powerful empires. And then Nebuchadnezzar, the fierce king of Babylon, who had defeated the Egyptians at Carchemish and Hama as well as all the sovereigns of Hatti and Phoenicia, besieged Jerusalem. The holy city was captured and pillaged.

It was 586 Before the Common Era.

More than ten thousand men were deported to Babylon. In exile, they remembered the one true God, a promise, and the wonders of earlier times. Words from the sky. A path through the sea.

With these ancient stories, they would write their hope.

I remember an ancient tale.

On the banks of the river of Babylon,
I sat down to cry.

I remember a very old story.
It begins long ago on the roads that lead
from Egypt to Mesopotamia.

I remember how we resisted the great kings
of Babylon and Assyria.

I remember Jerusalem.

I remember an ancient tale, which I will
tell you . . .

1.

Creation
or The First Words

based on *The Book of Genesis*, chapters 1 and 2

In the beginning God made the sky and the Earth,
the plants, the animals . . . and you and me.
And we learn why happiness lies
in naming the things of the world.
And how solitude was cured.

How it all began

we'll never know

But we have speech
And it is speech
that started it all

When all was dark
someone spoke
and light was made

When there was nothing, someone said
the words star, bear, tree
And a star, a bear, and a tree appeared

Everything is included in
the word of God
God wanted there to be something
rather than nothing

The land and the sea
The day and the night
The sun and the moon

Our world

The known and familiar world
And the unknown and distant one

It's the first page

Ten times God spoke.

The first time to say the words light and night, creating
a day.

The second time to separate the vault of the sky from the sea.

Day two.

The third time to separate the land from the sea.

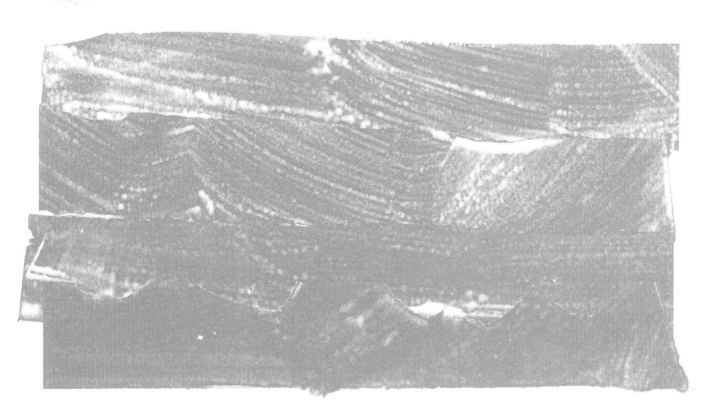

The fourth time to create
the plants and the trees.
Day three.

The fifth time to create the sun and
the moon and the stars in the sky.

Day four.

The sixth time to make a crowd
of living beings in the sea and
a crowd of flying ones to fill the sky.
Day five.

The seventh time to tell all beings
in water and sky to go forth and multiply.
The eighth time to give birth
to all that lives on land.
The ninth time to make an *adam*
in his image, both male and female,
and to make it the kind master
over all the fish, birds,
and animals of the Earth.
The tenth time to give
the plants to the animals
so they'd have something to eat.

Day six.

Relaxation and repose.
Day seven.

To name things well
increases the happiness of the world.

And then we begin counting the days.

We were alone in a vast, vast garden. With nothing and no one
that looked like us, no one to talk to, to laugh with, to love.
Or to fight with, or dream with . . .

No one to help us when we were afraid,
when we were lost, when we needed aid.

So God wondered what he could invent to ease our loneliness and distress.

Way at the end of the garden, deep in the shade,
out came a lion, and then a hyena,
then a grasshopper, a parrot, a horse . . .

Soon, there were animals and animals and animals.
And they all had to be named.

Some were more challenging than others . . .
All the beasts of the field and all the birds of the air paraded by.

Animals are sacred companions. Some are alarming. Others are quite sweet. And still others are a bit odd.

But no one. No one to talk to, to declare love to, to live with, to have children with, to get old with . . .

Meanwhile, all over the garden, the animals were having a great time. Them.

Better to go to sleep than to sit in a corner alone.

So God put us to sleep.

When we woke up, we were two.

She and he. She and I.

And the whole garden woke up like the sky.

2.

The Garden
or Why
Leave Paradise?

based on the *Book of Genesis*, chapter 3

In which we learn about the first steps of Adam and Eve, the heroes of good and evil, despite themselves. And why the dream came to an end. And how the door of the history of man opened before them.

In those days, the Earth was a garden like the gardens of Babylon.

A huge garden watered by four great rivers.

A garden full of fabulous fruit growing on beautiful trees.

In this great garden lived the man, Adam, and the woman, Eve.

They lived with the wolves and the lambs.

They lived among the lions and gazelles.

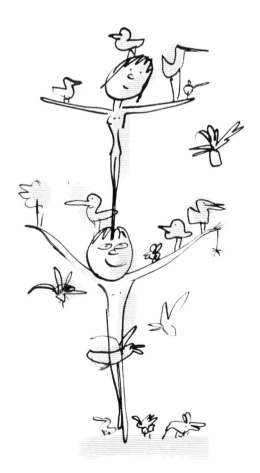

They lived with the birds and the smallest bugs.

To eat, they had only to gather the flowers and grasses.

And collect the fruit that fell to the ground.

And drink from the springs.

In those days, no one had ever heard of illness or death.
In those days, fear did not exist.

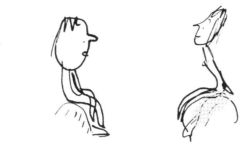

There was no shame.

In those days, no one worked. It was paradise.

In the middle of this great garden, there was a tree unlike all the others:
the tree of the knowledge of good and evil.

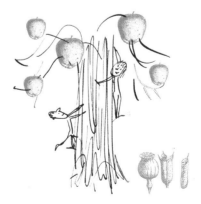

It was a tree to sit under and sleep and dream.
They could eat any fruit in the garden, except that from this tree.

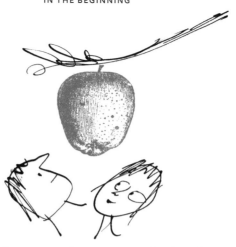

Marvelous fruit that the man and woman watched with an envious eye.
For it was said: *Ye shall not eat of it, neither shall ye touch it, lest ye die.*
It was the tree of adventure, the tree of desire.

The tree of all mysteries: birth and death,

growth and age,

work,

making babies . . .

The tree of all dreams: to grow beautiful and strong,

to travel far,

to succeed, to be loved . . .

The tree of all temptation: pleasure, love,

gambling, adventure, wealth . . .

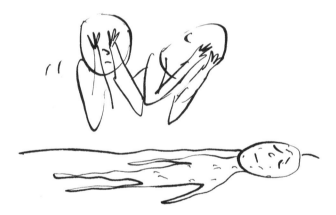

But also the tree of all distress: death,

poverty,

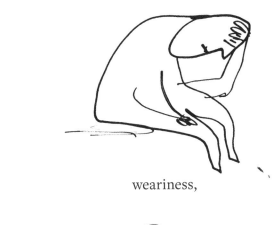

weariness,

war,

exile . . .

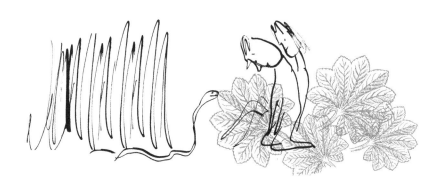

One day at the foot of the tree, there was a snake, sleek and naked, and he liked teasing them.

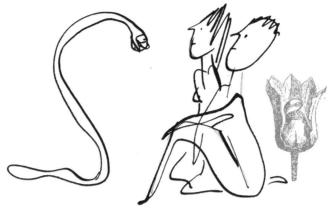

Eat this, and you'll be completely different.
You won't die, but it will open your eyes.

You'll see it all otherwise. The garden. And everything that lives here. The sky . . .

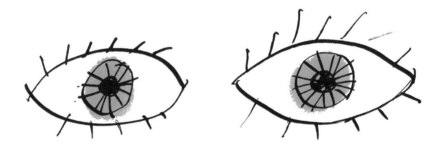

Eat this, and you'll be surprised, he said.

The temptation was too strong. Eve took one of the fruits. Adam wanted some too.

She gave him half.

Suddenly, they were afraid of the lion.

Suddenly, they were afraid of the spider, and the trees, and the clouds . . .

They ran and hid in the garden.

They wanted cover and dared not look at each other.

And the snake turned mean. He was clearly not their friend.

Then they heard a voice in the garden. God called out to Adam: Where are you?

I heard you in the garden, and I got scared; I'm naked, and I went to hide.

And he denounced the woman, saying: *She gave me of the tree and I did eat . . .*

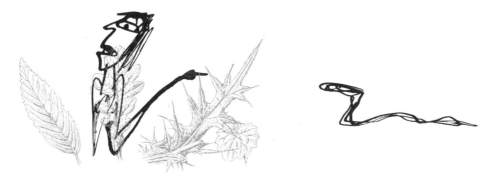

And the woman, in turn, blamed it all on the snake.

Whom God expelled: *Upon thy belly shalt thou go,* and dine on dust for the rest of your life.

And to the woman, he said: Giving birth will give you great pain,
and in your pain, you will bear sons. And man will be master over you.

And to the man: You must work for what you eat.

And you'll live on weeds. You'll get nothing but thistles and thorns from the Earth.

For dust thou art, and unto dust shalt thou return.

And the whole garden changed and became cruel,
full of thorns and thistles and briars and prickles.

Time to go. The dream was over.
The man and the woman opened the door into human history.

They were going to have to work, bear children, share with others,

wander the Earth, and love and hate, for generation after generation.

3.

Cain and Abel
or Murderous Jealousy

based on *The Book of Genesis*, chapter 4

In which we learn of the difficult beginnings of communal life. And how jealousy poisons relationships. And that the first crime was to kill a brother and that vengeance is not our own.

And it came to pass that they had to live together and everyone had to work.

Some of them tamed animals and raised them in the fields.

Others grew gardens full of delectable vegetables and delicious fruit.

But the more they worked, the more they grew proud of what they produced,

and so the more they argued. And became jealous of one another.

Among them were two brothers: Cain and Abel.

Cain, the older and stronger, worked the Earth.

Abel, the younger and weaker, watched over chickens, goats, and sheep in small herds.

One evening, they both brought the best that they had to offer to God.
Cain: a magnificent basket of fruit and vegetables.
Abel: baby chicks and lambs.

He had chosen the cutest.

Cain hung out in the shadows.

Away from the fun. No one paid any attention to him, nor to his vegetables and fruit.

Whereas Abel and his baby animals were a big hit.

Cain fumed.
Deep inside him was a beast ready to pounce upon his prey.

God asked: Why such a face? *Why art thou wroth?*

Cain wanted to talk to his brother, but he couldn't quite bring himself to.

He led him out into the fields of rich grain, wheat and rye . . .

They walked for a long time.

Abel said little.

He suddenly felt so small and weak.

And Cain set upon him and killed him.

And then the voice of God, demanding: Where is Abel, your brother?

Cain: Who knows?

All day, I work the fields; I don't have time to watch over others.

Again, God's voice: What have you done? Fear struck Cain to the bone.

The Earth turned red, red like the blood of his brother and that of all his sons.
And the fields, the grain, the stones, all started to shout.

Cain panicked and ran from the field.

Everyone stepped back to let him pass. All there gathered watched him flee.
Watched him run out of the country.

Cain was afraid of them. But they were also afraid of him. No one dared stop him.
No one dared strike him. There Cain went, crushed by the weight of his crime.

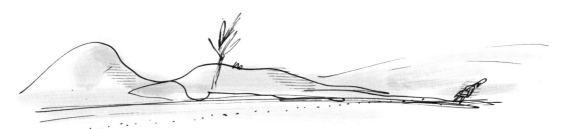

But God protected him and prevented anyone from killing him.
Cain walked alone, very far, as far as possible from anyone's sight.

He stopped one day just east of Eden. And there he sat down to rest.

And there he went back to living and working
and there with his wife had many, many children.

And there built the world's first city. For his numerous children all also had numerous children.
They became shepherds and nomads and forgers and musicians . . . They became the entire world.

4.

Noah
or The Last Temptation of God

based on *The Book of Genesis*, chapters 6 through 9

In which Noah brings two of every
creature on Earth into his ark to save them
from the great waters and learns that
he can now eat meat and dominate the
world and everything in it—and, in which
terrifying circumstances, we learn how
fragile we are.

The human race spread to cover the entire face of the Earth.
Just as God had commanded.

But strange things began to happen.
Things no one had ever imagined.

The extraordinary beauty of human girls turned heads.
And people started saying that giants and ogres were mixing with men.

Violence raged. Confusion reigned.

Wars were waged.

And ruin spread far and wide.

One man resisted. Remained apart. He was Noah.

A good man.

When God decided to wipe clean the surface of the Earth, he remembered him.
And said these strange words: *Make thee an ark*.

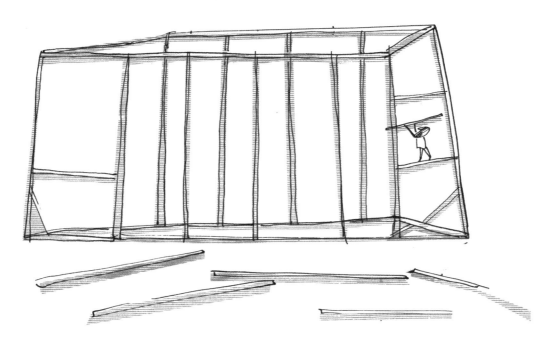

Yes, an ark with many rooms.

And a single enormous door. Make it three stories tall.

And God said: *Come thou and all thy house into the ark.*

And with you bring two of every living thing, every species on land and in the air.

Noah was six hundred years old.
And brought two of every thing alive into his boat.

From the biggest to the littlest.

And then a door in the sky opened up. It was the Flood.

It was a disaster.

A huge wave covered the Earth, over the tops of the mountains.

The water destroyed everything that had ever been made.
And all that lived upon the Earth.

Noah's boat sailed away.

Inside, Noah counted the days.

It went on forever.

From time to time, he sent out a dove to reconnoiter.

Three times he sent forth the bird, and on the third, it did not return.

The Earth was dry.

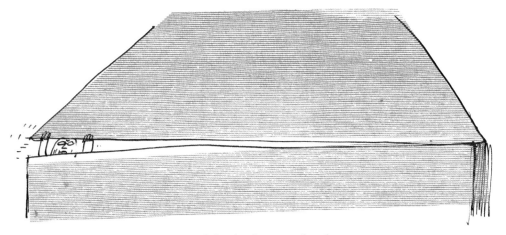

Noah looked out at the sky.

And saw that the door in it was shut.

The sun again warmed the land.

The Earth dried off and became like new.
With new meadows and new hills.

God remembered Noah and said: Come out of your ark.
Everyone came out and found solid ground, and light, and air.

The grasses and flowers had a new scent.
Everyone forgot the worst and began to live again.

God said: *Be fruitful, and multiply, and replenish the Earth.*
Never again will I destroy; I will think of you and keep my word.

But all animals will now run from you in fear

For from now on you may hunt them and eat their meat.

So, we began to live again, and to work and to love.

We began again to explore the Earth and sky.

And we began again to fight.

And again, we went to war.

Watch out, said God, *Whoso sheddeth man's blood, by man shall his blood be shed . . . and at the hand of every man's brother will I require the life of man.*

Noah, remembering God, planted the very first vine.
And picked and pressed the very first grape and drank the first glass of wine.

Something big had changed, but what?

Life had become so fragile.
And the Earth now seemed so small.

5.

Babel

or The Tale of Totalitarian Folly

based on *The Book of Genesis*, chapter 11

In which we learn the consequences
of the entire world deciding to live
together in a single tower and to speak
a single language in a single voice.

After the Flood, the human race again became so numerous that it spread out all over the Earth.

Creating many different peoples and many different nations.

And many different languages.

And the different peoples had different laws.

They weren't all headed in the same direction.
Either literally or figuratively.

Many were afraid of becoming scattered. They wanted to come together as one.

And speak only one language. And have only one voice.

So on the great plain of Babylon, they all stopped. And there, down they sat.

And said to each other: Let's make a bunch of bricks! And let's bake them!

And with them, let's make a great city. And with the city, make a great tower.

A tower so tall it will touch the stars.
And rival the sun and the moon.

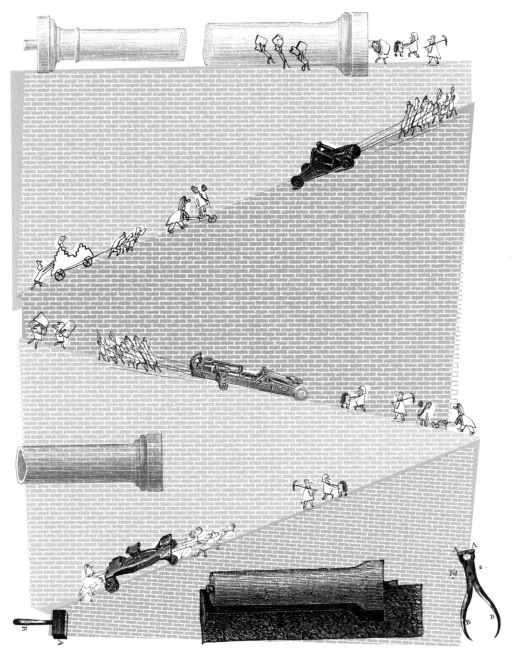

It was a big job.

The bricks to build the tower became more important, more precious, than human lives.

In this tower, they would all be together.

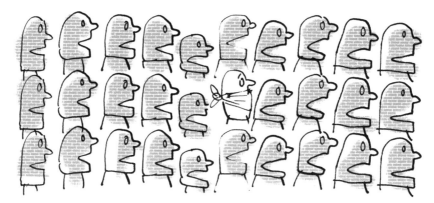

They would speak in a single voice. And their words would all be the same.

And there would be nothing they couldn't do.
It would be the tower of their wildest dreams—and of their thirst for power.

And everyone would understand each other.

So they added another story, and then another, and then another . . . up and up and up.

Until one day . . .
it all fell down.

The tower.

And their dreams of power . . .

All a complete mess.

God wanted humanity to cover the Earth,

speaking different languages.

So that they'd have to try really hard to understand each other.

And they all set off in different directions to wander.

And so there were different peoples. And different languages. And different hopes.
When they met on the roads, they had to struggle to grasp what they heard.
For though everyone was speaking, everyone was using new words.

6.

Abraham

or The Call
to Separation

based on *The Book of Genesis*, chapter 12

In which Abraham abandons everything
in order to respond to a mysterious call.
And we learn of the trials that drove him
all the way to Egypt—and we learn that
the first patriarch was ready to do pretty
much anything to save his own skin.

They'd all been scattered.
Noah's children, and Noah's children's children.

They'd crossed deserts, forded rivers, followed stars.

There were Shem and Arphaxad. There were Japheth and Eber.
There were Peleg and Reu. There were Nahor and Terah . . .

All of them had walked and walked.

And there was Abraham.

One night, Abraham was lying under the stars. He couldn't sleep.

He heard a voice he'd never heard before.

The voice said: Leave. Leave your native land.
Leave your family and everything you own.

And I will make of thee a great nation,
and that great nation shall be your home.

Abraham heard the promise and rose.

That night he said goodbye to all that he knew.
Goodbye to his family, goodbye to his friends, goodbye to his good name.

With him, he took his wife, Sarah, and Lot, his brother's son.

He began a voyage from which he would never return.

He had been told to change his life.

The trip seemed endless. Border crossings.
Checkpoints. Wrong turns. Hunger and thirst.

Freezing nights.

Hostile towns.

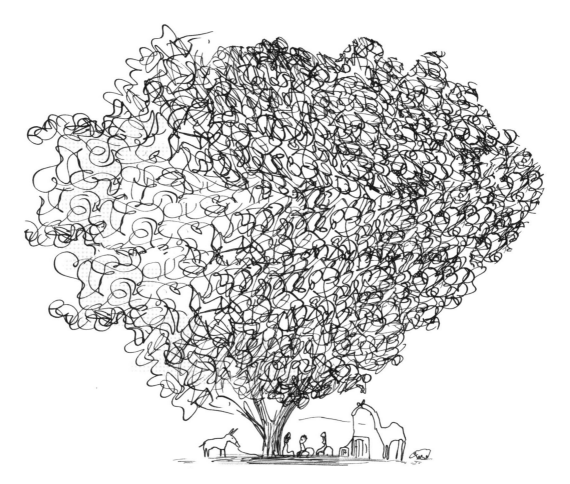

One night, they stopped at Sichem. Under a great tree.

In the dim light, they thought they were alone.

But no, people already lived there. They would never find a place of their own.

But Abraham heard God say: *Unto thy seed have I given this land.*

So there he pitched his tent.

And built an altar to God to remind him of what he'd said.

Next day: Strike camp and move on.

And on it went: Pitch the tent and take it down, night after night, day after day.

While famine ravaged the land.

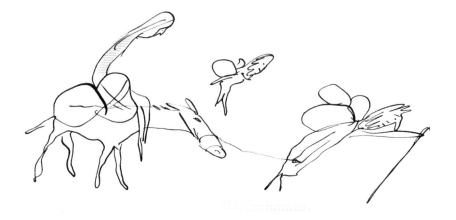

And Abraham, frightened, fled farther away.

And finally found himself in Egypt.

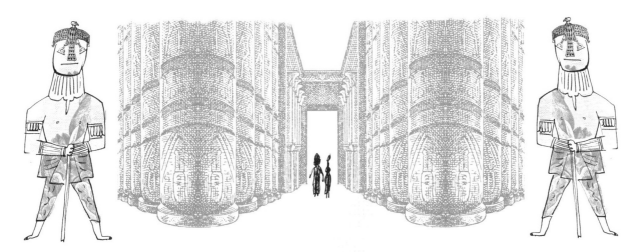

Where there, too, the Pharaoh's guards filled him with fear.

His wife was so lovely, so lovely; the Pharaoh would take her.
And kill him in return.

So Abraham told the Pharaoh that Sarah was not his wife, but his sister.

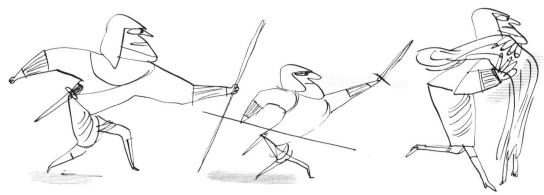

The Pharaoh was overwhelmed—Sarah, so lovely, so lovely…
he grabbed her and brought her to his palace.

And in exchange, he gave Abraham donkeys, camels, sheep, servants, and gold and silver . . .

While Sarah was left locked up with the Pharaoh.

Abraham held his tongue.

But in the end, the penny dropped: She was not his sister.

So we find Abraham exiled once more.

Back on the road.

Taking all he earned in Egypt along.
As well as his Sarah, so lovely, so loved.

7.

Abraham and Sarah

or Laughter Made Flesh

based on *The Book of Genesis*, chapters 17 and 18

In which there is much laughter following statements made by visiting foreigners. And we see the results of these incredulous and impetuous outbursts.

It had been so long since Abraham and Sarah had left their land.
Now they were foreigners wherever they went.

But they had been promised a country of their own.

A promise is an invisible country on which to make a stand.

Abraham looked up at the star-studded sky, and kept the promise in mind:

One day, he'd have more children than there are stars in the sky.

And God said: *I will give unto thee, and to thy seed after thee, the land wherein thou art a stranger.*

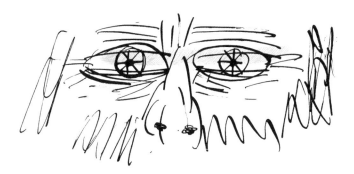

And on top of that, I'll make this pact: You'll have a son with Sarah.

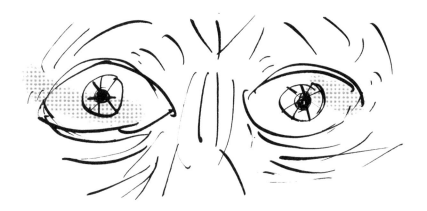

And you will call him Isaac, meaning "He who laughs."

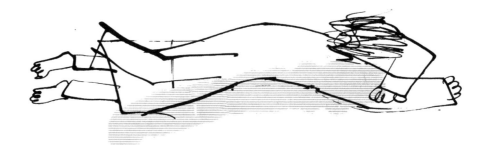

And Abraham fell down laughing.

You could hear him laughing from one end of the country to the other.

A child? Him? Impossible!

He was ninety-nine years old!

And his wife, Sarah, was ninety!

How could they possibly have a son?

This was truly a laughing matter.

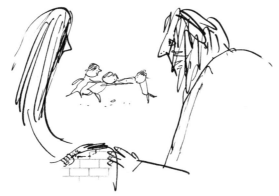

And anyway, they already had Ishmael,
the son that Abraham had had with their servant Hagar.

At that very moment, Ishmael was playing with the other children in the camp.

Abraham adored him and ardently watched over him.

The next day, as the sun was at its height, Abraham lay down under the tree of Sichem.

When three strangers suddenly appeared.

They'd come a long, long way. They were thirsty and hungry.

Abraham didn't think twice. He welcomed them warmly.

And asking nothing, he begged them to stay the night.

Everyone got busy.

In the tent, Sarah cooked up a meal—milk, cakes, veal.

Outside, all was arranged for the feast.

Evening found them gathered around a table under a tree.

Sarah—ear out on a stick—listened in to what they said.

The strangers told Abraham they'd be back in a year ... when Sarah would have a newborn child!

The old woman slipped into the tent and started to laugh.

A laugh full of all that had been lost.

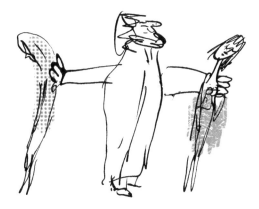

Lost hopes.

Hopeless promises.

Suddenly, the impossible had burst in and started knocking on the door of her life.

Sarah reneged. Frightened. No, I didn't laugh, she said.

But from the shadows, a voice said: Yes, you did.

Yes, you laughed. And from that laugh, the impossible was born. The unforeseen.

A promise suddenly, right before your eyes, became a real thing.

A smile that turned into a tiny child: Isaac.

God taught me to laugh, said Sarah, and I welcome it.

8.

Sodom

or Devastating Inhospitality

based on *The Book of Genesis*, chapter 19

In which Abraham, faced with the anger of God, becomes an advocate for the people of Sodom, and we learn that the Sodomites' crime is not exactly the one we thought it was.

Abraham and his nephew Lot returned from Egypt.

They were rich and numerous.

They went back to the land that they'd been promised.

But it didn't work out.

It was already inhabited.

The atmosphere was competitive.

Walls were built.

Fights broke out.

Rich and numerous, yes, but unable to live in peace.

Each went his own way.

Lot opened his eyes and looked around.

Far off across the plain, he saw a magnificent city sparkling with gardens.

And a little farther on, a tiny little no-account town.

Lot and his crew went off to live in Sodom.

But in the enormity of Sodom, one could get lost, to say the least.

Everyone just laughed when Lot said to his people: God is threatening to destroy the city.

Abraham remained apart. He stayed good.

On the road to the promise, there are difficult choices to be made.

Abraham stood his ground. But God was worried about him. Very worried.

Abraham did not want Sodom to be destroyed.

He was ready to drive a hard bargain with God.

Abraham said: Before you *I am but dust and ashes.*

But you'll kill good people along with the bad.

Really? said God. Just how many good people do you think there are?

50, 45, 40, 30, 20, 10 . . .

God listened to Abraham.
Even for ten innocent people, he would not destroy Sodom.

Abraham, once more, found himself alone.

He wanted to run after God and catch him,

and plead with him some more . . .

But he found he couldn't budge.

How could he save the city?

In Sodom, violence was all the rage. They hunted down foreigners, anyone who was different.

Lot opened his doors to two strangers being chased by a crowd

that wanted to lynch them.

The crowd banged on Lot's door.

But Lot refused to hand them over.

Hospitality is unconditional. There is no wiggle room!

Just to make himself perfectly clear,
Lot went as far as to say that he'd prefer to hand over his own daughters.

It was night. The city began to quake. Out went all the lights.

Lot took fright and fled.

Behind him, everything was razed. The city, its people, its trees.
And fire rained down upon the plain.

Everyone ran,
foreigners as well as Sodomites,
travelers as well as residents,
all on the road, running from the ruin.

9.

Abraham and Isaac

or The Test of the Ties of Blood

based on *The Book of Genesis*, chapter 22

In which Isaac thinks his final hour has
come as his father obeys an obscure but
divine command, and we learn that life
and death depend on the interpretation
of orders from the sky.

One day, they had to set off again.

The voice, the same one, called to Abraham on the evening wind.

Here I am.

Abraham was always there when the voice called.

Take now thy son, thine only Isaac, whom thou lovest

and head for those mountains you see in the distance.

Abraham obeyed.

But did he really hear the voice say *that*?
Sometimes obeying just makes you more alone.

The sun rose.

Abraham did too.

And saddled his horse.

He chopped the wood for the sacrificial fire.

He took his son Isaac and two other boys.

And started for the mountain that God had mentioned.

Once at its foot, they split up.

Abraham and Isaac would climb the mountain alone.

Abide ye here with the ass, said Abraham to the boys.

We'll be right back.

En route, Isaac started getting a bit nervous.

It was certainly a very long way.

And where was the sacrificial lamb?

Worry not, his father told him.

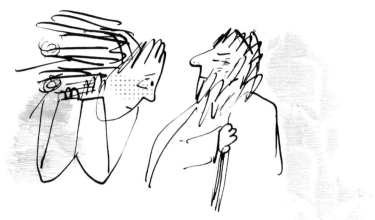

Isaac obeyed his father as his father obeyed God.

And he felt more and more alone on the path, as had his father.

At the top of the mountain, time stopped.

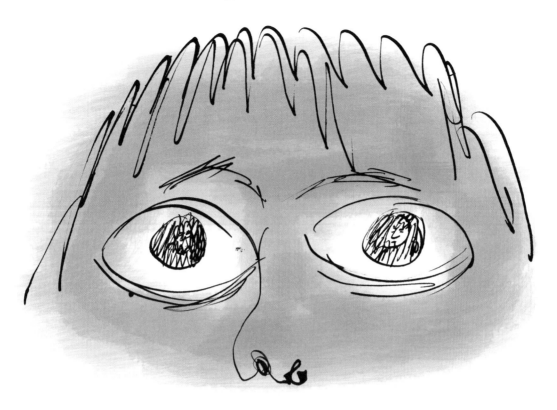

All was dark.

Abraham built the fire.

And took Isaac, his cherished son, and tied him up.

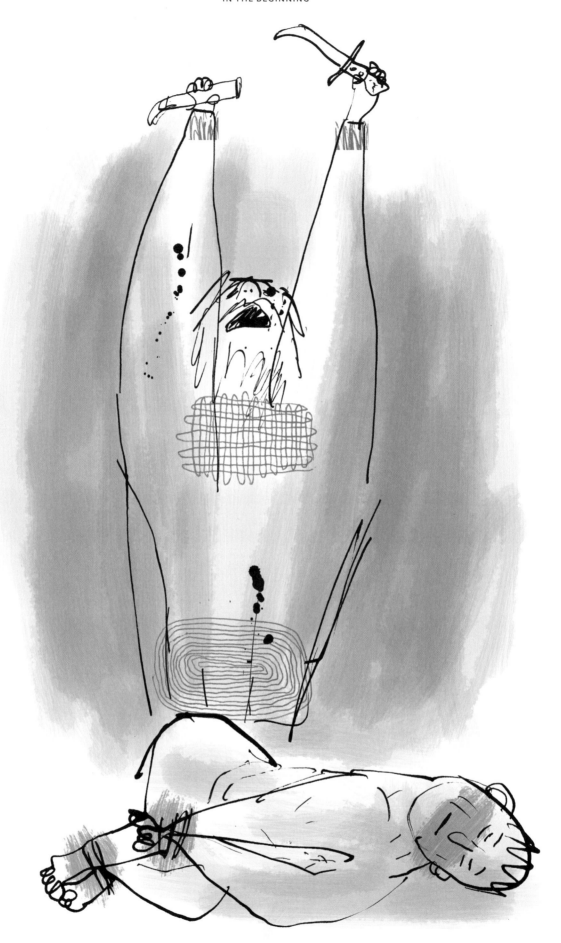

And took out his knife.

But wait! Once again, it was the voice.

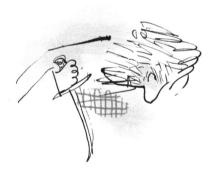

Here I am.

Abraham raised his eyes and saw the ram.

And consequently saw the light.

He freed his cherished son.

You're never more alone than when you're in the dark.

Isaac took his father in his arms. They embraced and then moved apart.

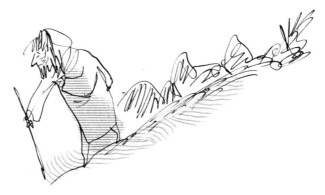

Abraham walked back down the mountain alone to join the others.

It was night. Stars overflowed the infinite sky.

And at that moment, he, too, felt freed. Though he had grown much older

Abraham felt young forever.

10.

Jacob and Esau

or The Bite of Reconciliation

based on *The Book of Genesis*, chapters 26 and 27

In which we hear the incredible story
of twin brothers turned enemies and
of Jacob, his mother's favorite, who became
an orphan on the roads of exile.

Isaac was thrilled. He couldn't believe it.

Rebecca's belly was growing like a happy hill.

And moving.

But Rebecca was a bit concerned.

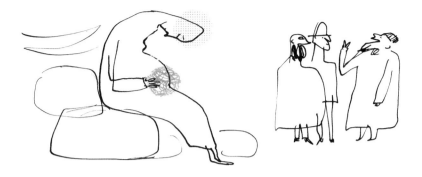

The twins were already at war in her womb.

Rebecca asked God about it, and he replied enigmatically: *The elder shall serve the younger.*

Jacob was born second *and his hand took hold on Esau's heel.*

From birth, one was strong and the other weak.

The strong one was Esau. He had bright red hair and was furry as a beast.

He loved to hunt, spending his time in the woods and fields.

Isaac liked him best.

They both loved huge feasts.

And Jacob was the weak.

He whiled away the time in his tent or outside, gazing at the stars.

His mother, Rebecca, loved him most.

They grew up, Jacob always smaller, Esau always stronger.

Their differences came between them.
Neither brother liked to admit that the other had his points.

One evening, Esau came back from the hunt.

He was dying of hunger.

Before him, a delicious plate of red lentils.

Jacob said to him: Dig right in, but in exchange, *sell me this day thy birthright.*
I'll be the older. And I'll be the stronger.

Esau said yes—anything, as long as he could eat and drink!

And it came to pass that Isaac's family grew to a considerable size.

Wherever he went, Isaac saw wells that his father, Abraham, had dug.

The Quarrel wells.

The Liberty wells.

The Promise wells.

Trouble increased throughout the land. Isaac became a burden.

He became old, very old.

He could no longer see.

One last time, before he died, he wanted to eat a good meal with his son Esau.
And bless him.

But when the evening came, Rebecca wrapped Jacob in the skin of a goat.

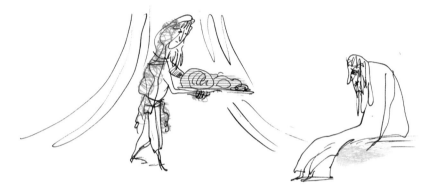

It was Jacob who entered the room with a plate of scrumptious game.

The blind old man reached out his hand to touch his son. A true animal's skin.

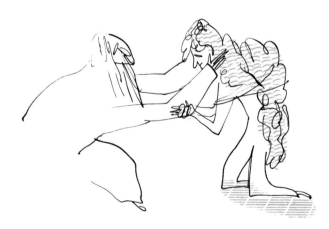

That's my Esau, he thought.

And thinking he was blessing Esau, Isaac blessed Jacob instead.

As Rebecca stood behind the door and watched the whole thing.
It was she who had disguised her son, and she who had cooked the meal.

Thief! cried Esau, when he came in from the hunt.
Jacob had stolen his blessing. Jacob had taken his place.

Behold, I have made him thy lord, confirmed Isaac, old and trembling.
A word once given cannot be taken back.

Esau cried.

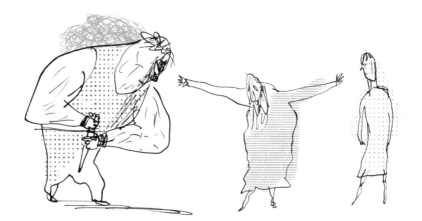

He would kill his brother—that he swore.

And so once more, better that each go off on his own.

Jacob went into exile, far from brother and home.

Rebecca lamented.

She wanted both of her children.

But how could the two brothers ever be reconciled?

11.

Jacob's Battle

or Hand-to-Hand Combat with God

based on *The Book of Genesis*, chapters 32 and 33

In which the story of Jacob continues
with a door opening in the sky and a
midnight fight with a mysterious being
rising up from a dream. And he finds
himself finally in his brother's arms.

Since leaving his brother, Jacob had lived in darkness.
Darkness and fear.

Jacob was fleeing his brother's vengeance.

To appease him, he sent him two hundred goats, twenty rams, two hundred sheep . . .

Esau refused them all.

Jacob went into hiding.

Deep in the abyss.

Where, in the dark of night, he dreamt.

And in his dream, he saw a ladder come down from the sky.

With angels on every rung, going down to the very bottom, and then back up again into the light. Passing each other as they went. Each one carrying a bit of night up to heaven and bringing a bit of heaven back down into the night.

Jacob heard the voice of God: *I am with thee,*

and I will not leave thee.

He woke up in a cold sweat.

He felt so small.

It was the gate of Heaven! Here on Earth, and open!

Jacob raised a great stone in remembrance of this dream

and swore fidelity to the house of God if he returned safely home.

And then one day at dusk, he came to the banks of a great river with his flocks.
They had to cross before nightfall.

Jacob crossed last.

He remained alone while the others made camp farther down the bank.

Someone was waiting, there in the shadows

to fight him throughout the night.

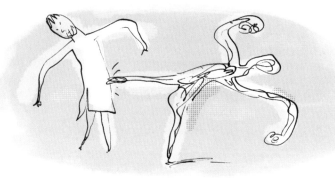

Though injured in the hip and beginning to limp,

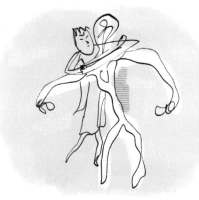

the thrilled and terrified Jacob proved the stronger.

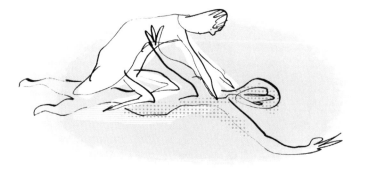

He was fighting to discover the name of the other in the dark. He fought to see his face.

The sun rose.

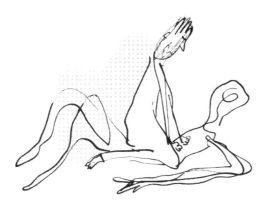

The stranger asked to be released. Jacob said: Only if you bless me.

"What is your name?" asked the stranger.
Jacob.

Thy name shall be called no more Jacob, but Israel.

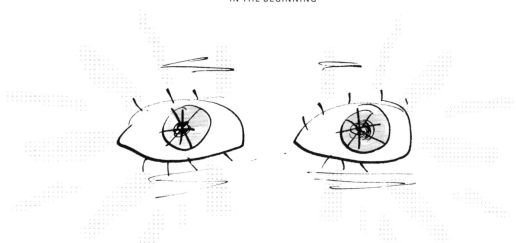

Jacob had seen the face of God.

One evening, he looked up and saw, on the far horizon, dust in a great cloud.

A messenger ran up to say: It's Esau, at the head of an army of four hundred men . . .

Jacob lay awake all night. Scared.

Esau was coming to take his sworn revenge.

At dawn, the two brothers stood face to face across a great expanse.

Esau advanced.

He was alone.

Faster and faster he came, running, now full speed ahead.

And threw himself into his brother's arms, and they embraced.

A kiss or a bite?

The burning scar of pardon struck the two brothers speechless.

They cried. And though kindly, Esau refused Jacob's invitation to stay.

And so they went their separate ways.

12.

Joseph in Egypt
or The Man Who Dreamed

based on *The Book of Genesis*, chapters 37 through 41

In which Joseph, the son of Jacob, persecuted by his brothers, finds refuge in Egypt, where he prospers, going from prison into the Pharaoh's court.

One day, Joseph, the son of Jacob, was out wandering in the hills.

Clearly searching, he went from camp to camp.

And to everyone—nomads, robins, sheep, and lambs: Have you seen my brothers? he asked.

I am looking for my brothers.

Everyone noticed him because he was wearing a splendid coat of many colors.

Mr. Dreamer!

Look at him! Thinking he sparkles like the stars!

Suddenly, there were all of his brothers, crying: *Behold, this dreamer cometh!*

Mr. Dreamer with his head in the clouds and his mind in the moon.
Imagining glory.

They wanted to kill those dreams. And oust the dreamer.
The father's love had engendered the brothers' hatred.

They abandoned their flocks and threw themselves upon him.

They tore off his beautiful robe.

And stained it with the blood of a goat.
Which they would then show their father as proof that Joseph was gone forever.

And then they popped him down an empty well.

And so we find Joseph at the bottom of a pit, forgotten. Asking into the darkness:
Where are my brothers? And no longer dreaming, but thinking only of his father, Jacob.

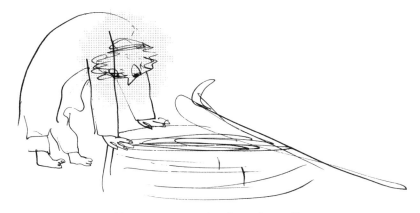

Ruben, Jacob's oldest son, went back to the well—
he didn't want his little brother killed. But Joseph was gone.

Nothing but the bloody robe remained.
Which he took back to his father.

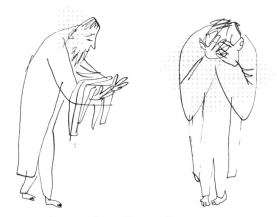

Who saw it and burst into tears.

Better to join Joseph in death, he said.

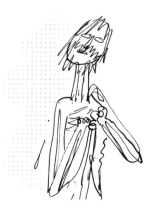

And Jacob rent his clothes, and put sackcloth upon his loins,

and mourned for his son many days.

But, in fact, his other brothers had plucked Joseph from the well
and sold him to a passing caravan headed for Egypt.

Where he was in turn sold to Potiphar, head honcho in the Pharaoh's administration.

And there we have it: Mr. Dreamer, a slave in Egypt . . .

But protected by God's shadow.
And the powerful Potiphar couldn't help but notice this.

And on this basis made Joseph his friend and counselor.
Gave him keys to his palace and made him guardian of all his goods.

Joseph had come into his own, the honor and envy of all.

Including Potiphar's extremely seductive wife.

Every day, as soon as her husband was out of sight,
she slithered suggestively up to Joseph, saying: *Lie with me.*

Then one night, she threw herself upon him and tore off his clothes.

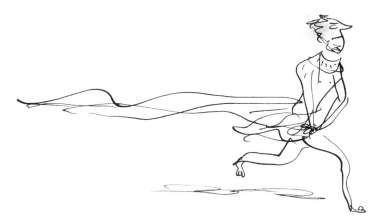

Joseph, not wanting to betray his patron, fled.

The princess called for help, claiming that Joseph had tried to rape her,
holding up his clothes as proof.

And yet again, we find Joseph unjustly imprisoned.

He who had been so high had been brought so brutally low.

Mr. Dreamer spent the next two years languishing in a dungeon with the head baker and the head cupbearer. At night, he'd look out the tiny basement window, and contemplate the moon and the stars. And he'd listen to his fellow prisoners' dreams and interpret them.

One day the door of the prison opened.

Joseph was needed. Every night, the Pharaoh dreamed astonishing things. But no one, neither magician nor wise man, could correctly interpret them.

Joseph shaved. Changed. Donned a flowing Egyptian robe.

Nightly, the Pharaoh went down to the Nile to sleep and dream.

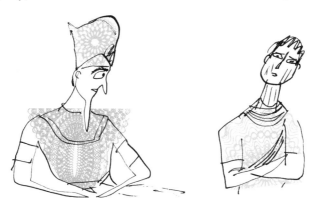

The Pharaoh told his dreams to Joseph.

Seven fat, sleek cows came out of the Nile.
Followed by seven skinny, ugly cows who devoured them.

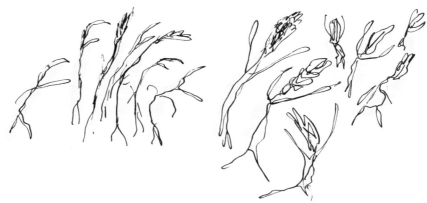

And then seven plump heads of grain, destroyed by seven shriveled ones scorched by wind.

Joseph saw it all instantly: *God hath shewed Pharaoh what he is about to do.*
There will be seven years of plenty followed by seven years of famine.

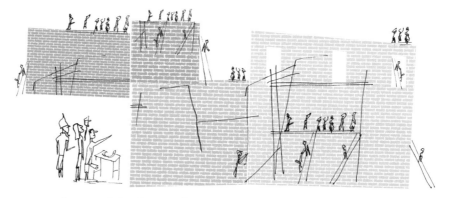

So Joseph built storehouses throughout all of Egypt.

During the seven good years, the grain was stored away.

Every peasant, every farmer brought Joseph a portion of his harvest.

Joseph had more wheat than there are grains of sand under the sea.

In thanks, the Pharaoh gave all he had to Joseph—his palace, his people, his robes, his jewels.

And for a wife, Asenath, the daughter of Potipherah, the priest of On.

The Pharaoh kept nothing but his throne.

When the seven years of famine hit, the people asked for food.
Go find Joseph and his storehouses, the Pharaoh said.

Starving by the thousands, the crowds descended upon Joseph.
No one will die, he promised.

He opened wide his storehouse doors and fed all the people of Egypt.
Who bowed down before him.

13.

Joseph and His Brothers

or The Man Who Fraternized

based on *The Book of Genesis*, chapters 42 through 45

In which Joseph saves his brothers
from the famine and we learn how,
through an amazing reversal of events,
evil can be turned into good.

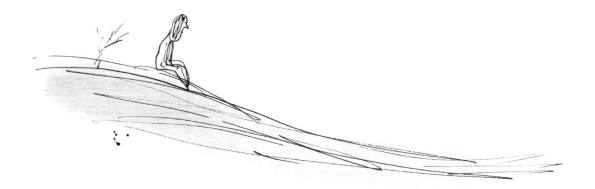

Joseph, Jacob's cherished son, had never been seen again.

Jacob lived alone with his grief and with Joseph as a memory.

The youngest, Benjamin, was the only son who still lived with him.

And famine ravaged the country.

One morning, the other ten brothers left for Egypt in search of food.

They'd heard that there they had huge warehouses full of grain.

And that a powerful man was, alone, feeding the whole nation.

It was to this man that Joseph's ten brothers appealed, starving and exhausted from their travels.

The man recognized his brothers at once, but didn't say a thing.
They, on the other hand, didn't recognize him in his new role as the great Egyptian.

The man accused them: *Ye are spies!*

And threw them all in prison for three days.

Which reminded them of their brother Joseph, and how they'd abandoned him.
He was just a child, and we were so cruel, they cried. Suddenly, how they missed him!

Day three: The door of the dungeon opened.

And Joseph proposed a curious deal.

I will set you free and give you all you need to eat.
For you and all your families.

But I will keep one of you, hostage, and so to remain here . . .

until you return ... and *bring your youngest brother unto me,*

so shall your words be verified, and ye shall not die.

Simon was the brother that stayed behind.

The nine others went back to their father, laden with grain, but heavy in heart.

But Jacob took one look at the deal and said no.

Joseph was gone, probably eaten by wild beasts.

Simon was in prison.

And now they expected him to give up Benjamin, too?

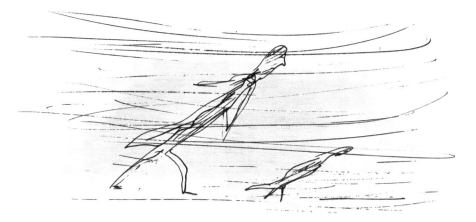

And yet famine raged on throughout the land.

And of all that food his sons had brought back, there was nothing left.

They'd have to return, and this time with Benjamin.

Jacob was heartbroken.

He cried, alone, in his empty house.

While in his grand palace, Joseph asked his brothers: How is your father?

And at the sight of the youngest, he turned his face aside and cried.

By hook or by crook, he wouldn't let Benjamin go.
He'd hide a gold cup in this baggage and accuse him of theft, and thus keep him with him in Egypt.

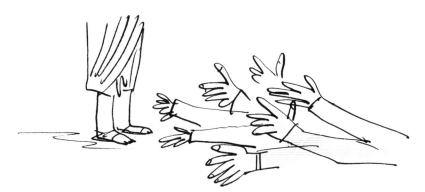

But the brothers begged him to let them take Benjamin back with them.

Losing him was something their father just could not bear.
His grief was already so great, casting him into the depths of despair.

The man listened in silence.

And then came closer and spoke:

I am Joseph your brother.
Whom ye sold into Egypt.

They were terrified.

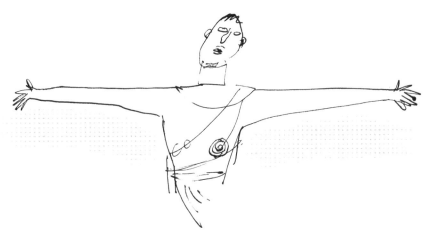

Now therefore not be grieved

for it was not you that sent me hither, but God. And he did so to save lives.

But how from evil can goodness arise?

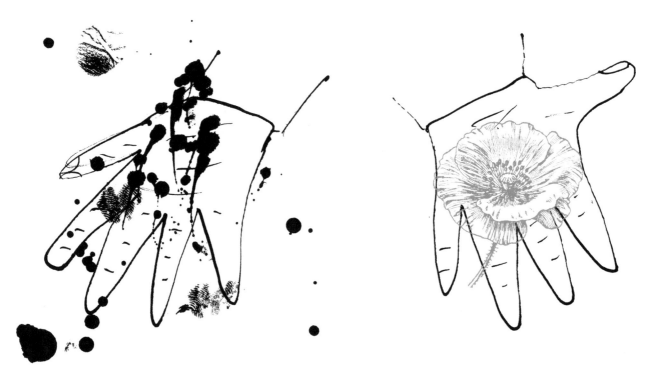

By seeing the evil that one has done. And by forgiving the evil done unto us.

Finally, one evening, Jacob, old and lonely, saw his sons' caravan in the distance, coming.

Bringing twenty donkeys laden with grain and bread and all good things.

And his sons announced: Joseph, our brother, your son, is in Egypt, alive and waiting for you.

And so, slowly, Jacob's heart came out of the dark.

And they all went down to Egypt to join Joseph and to build new lives. From their dreams.

14.

Moses

or The First to Learn the Name of God

based on *The Book of Exodus*, chapters 1 through 4

In which God chooses Moses to deliver his people from bondage and, in extraordinary circumstances, reveals himself in fire.

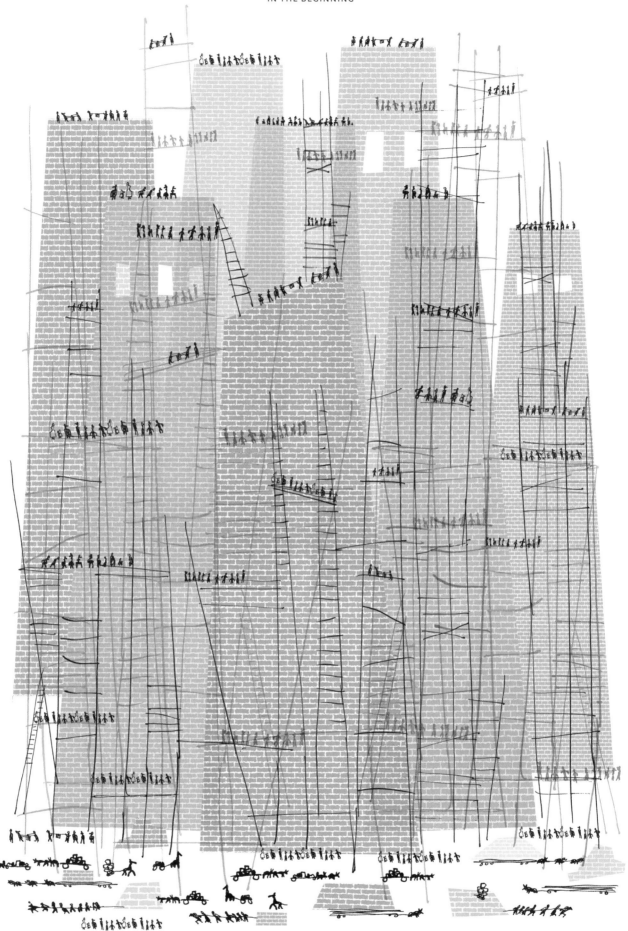

And it came to pass that they were building vast cities in Egypt. Under the Pharaoh's orders.

They beat and brutalized thousands of workers to get them to move the huge blocks of stone.

The Pharaoh always needed more workers.

So they made the Hebrews slaves.

And the Hebrews thrived.

The Hebrews are going to take over! said the Egyptians.

Fear and suspicion replaced peace and harmony. Hospitality gave way to hostility.

Until finally, the Pharaoh ordered the murder of all newborn Hebrew males.

He sent out the army with a single order:

Throw them into the Nile!

In those days, the Nile was a pretty busy place.
Crocodiles, fishing boats, fish, and glorious ships.

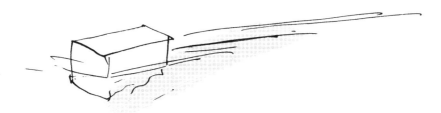

One day, on the green waters of the river, an odd little box floated by.

It worked its way slowly down through the reeds.

The Pharaoh's daughter was bathing near the bank.

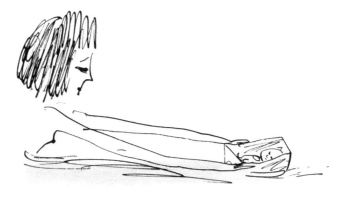

And saw the little box, going on its way.

Inside, she found a baby boy, crying but alive.
It was a Hebrew child.

The princess saved him from the waters.

She called him Moses and raised him with a nurse in the Pharaoh's court.

Moses the Egyptian grew up in sight of the suffering of the Hebrews, his true brothers, now enslaved.

And saw that there were two people to whom he belonged.

And it came to pass that he defended a Hebrew being beaten.

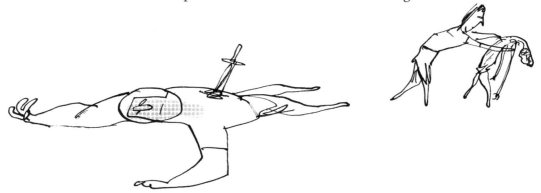

And killed the guard who was beating him.

Bad move. Moses had to flee. He went to live with the shepherds and their sheep.

One day while tending his flock, Moses noticed a little bush in flames.

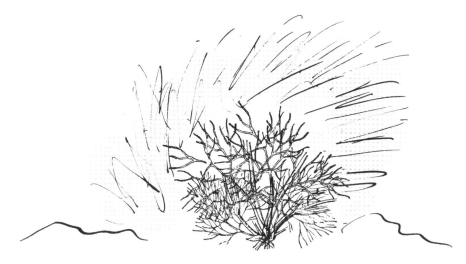

The fire lit the bush and warmed it up.

Here was fire that burned and yet did not destroy!

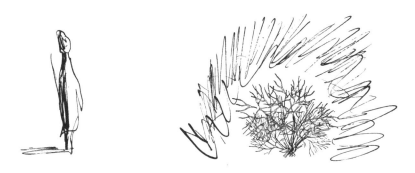

Instead of killing life, it shed light on it.

Moses, Moses, said the fire.

Here I am, he replied.

Draw not nigh hither, said the voice.

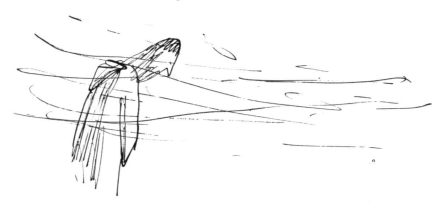

I have heard the children of Israel and their cries. I have seen how they suffer.
I have seen the slavery and the tyranny.

You must say to the Pharaoh: Let my people go.

And there I will be, with you.

To which Moses replied: But who are you?

I am the God of thy father, the God of Abraham, the God of Isaac, and the God of Jacob.

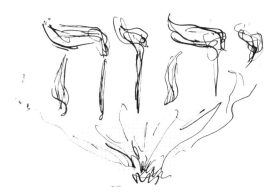

It is I, Yhwh.
I AM THAT I AM. The name that saves and frees.

Moses hid behind his face. Now hope had a name.

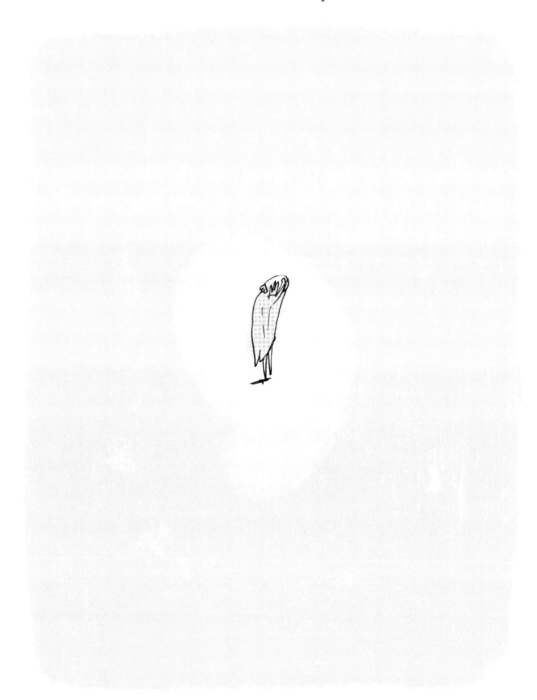

But he wasn't sure he could face it—the others would never believe him.

Cast down your staff, said the voice.

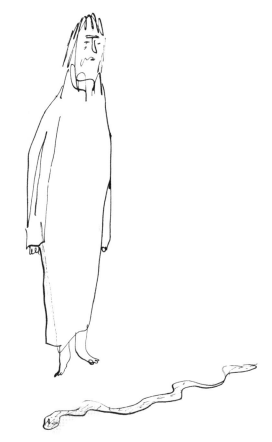

And it became a snake.

But the others, in fact, wouldn't listen, and he didn't know what else to say.
I will be with thy mouth, and teach thee what thou shalt say, said the voice.

15.

The Liberation of the People

or The Night of the Passage

based on *The Book of Exodus*, chapters 9 through 15

In which Moses and the Pharaoh engage
in a power struggle, and the people, in the
middle of the night, learn of their liberation
and, later, of the price of freedom.

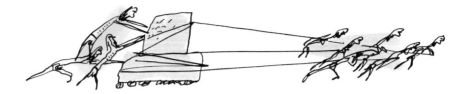

For four hundred years, on the Pharaoh's work sites, the people were enslaved.

Every day, no matter what, they had to make the same number of bricks.

Bricks of fear. Bricks of shame.

Each day, Moses and his brother Aaron went to the palace to talk with the Pharaoh.

They told him: *Thus saith the Lord God of the Hebrews: Let my people go.*

But the Pharaoh said no: Work or die.

Moses defied the Pharaoh and all his magicians and sorcerers.

Aaron threw his stick on the ground, and it turned into a snake.

The pharaoh's magicians laughed and did the same.

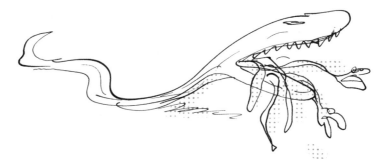

But Aaron's snake ate all the others up.

And yet still the Pharaoh would not give in.

To work! To work! cried the Hebrew slave drivers.
Don't listen to Moses. It's because of him that they hate us.

Moses was desperate. He said to God: Since I spoke to the Pharaoh in your name, it's only gotten
worse. Even my own people will no longer listen; why on Earth should the Pharaoh?

And God said: Got it! The Pharaoh's heart will I harden.

Rivers of blood.

Plagues of frogs, mosquitoes, and vermin.

All the livestock died.

Boils.

Hail.

Plagues of locusts.

Night all over.

Every time disaster struck, the Pharaoh grew frightened and called for Moses.
And yet every time, the Pharaoh felt his heart getting harder and harder.

The tyrant who won't hear the pain of his victims also eventually can't hear his own.

The Pharaoh became, in turn, a victim of his own violence.

At last, before the great exodus, there came the final blow.
The ultimate disaster that would make the Pharaoh give in.

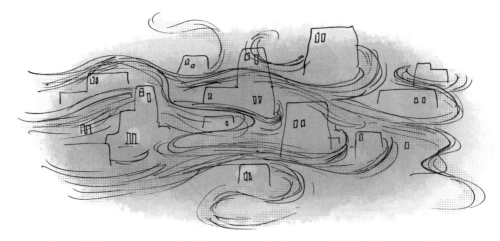

One night, rampant death beneath the doors of all the houses slid,

killing the firstborn of every family. Rich and poor. Prince and slave. Man and beast.

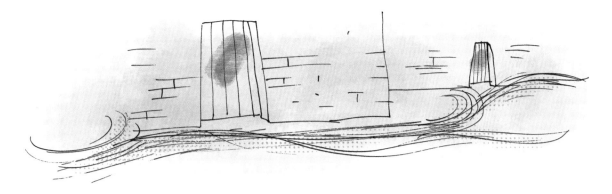

But the breath of death passed right by the doors of the Hebrews and did not come in.
They had all marked their doors with the blood of a lamb, as God had instructed them.

The lamb and the bread that they ate in haste, before it could rise, as they hurried to leave

As night fell and their great exodus began.

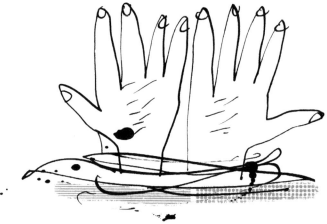

It was Passover. The great departure. Freedom—and a leap into the unknown.

God said to each one: *And this day shall be unto you for a memorial.* Remember it.

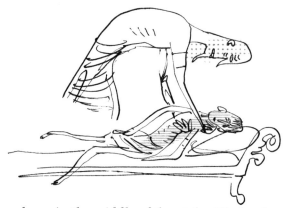

The Pharaoh woke up in the middle of the night. His firstborn son was dead.

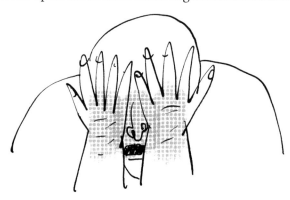

All Egypt was a single cry of grief. Not a house, not a palace, without a dead child.

The Pharaoh's heart was in shreds. He freed all the slaves. And let Moses and his people go.

During the day, they were led through the desert by a pillar of cloud.

At night, by a pillar of fire.

The Hebrews brought with them everything precious.
And Moses carried the bones of Joseph.

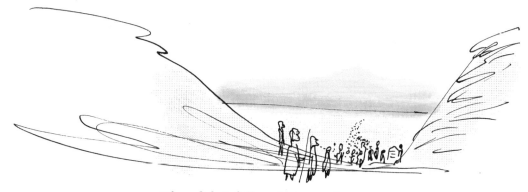

They didn't follow their usual route
But walked into the unknown. Straight toward the sea.

The people grew frightened and cried: Better a slave in Egypt than dead in the desert!

Fear not, said Moses, God is with us.

There before the great sea, the night brightened. Moses raised his staff.
And the sea parted, just as God had parted the waters from the land at the beginning of the world.
The liberated people walked away between the two walls of water.

Mad with grief and vengeance, the Pharaoh sent his armies after the fleeing people.

But the walls closed in on them. Horses and riders, engulfed in the waters.

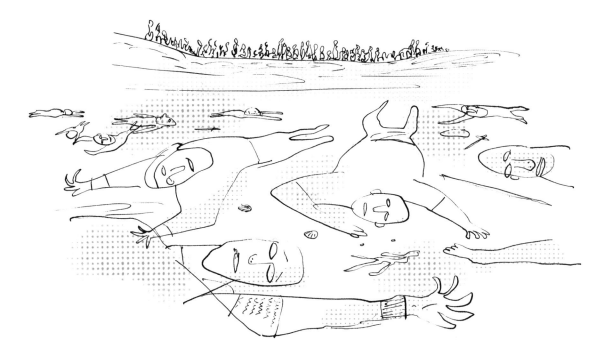

Free at last, the Hebrews turned back to see the Egyptian dead scattered all over the far bank.

And in front of them, the desert.
And through it, the path to freedom, and to responsibility.

16.

The Ten Commandments

or The Paths to Liberty

based on *The Book of Exodus*, chapters 16 through 31

In which manna falls from heaven and ten laws come from a smoking, shaking mountain. And responsibility proves a difficult apprenticeship.

Free at last.
Slavery in Egypt was now just a bad memory, and yet the people were worried.

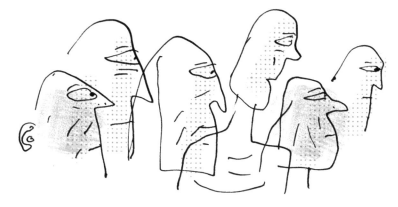

Ahead of them, nothing. The desert. What now?

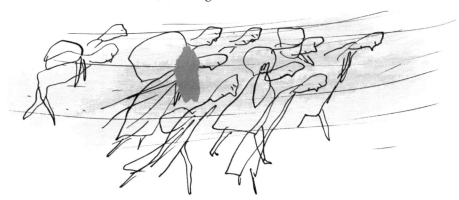

A desert engenders all kinds of fears and frustrations.
There's nothing there! The wait was long. The days were scalding. And the nights freezing.

How can you become a free people under such conditions?

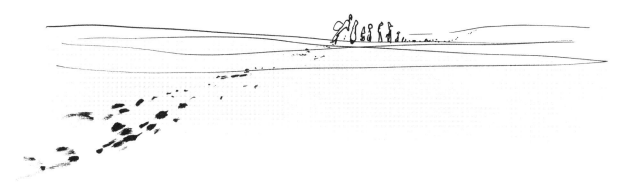

But the passage through the desert was their apprenticeship in liberty and responsibility.

The people started arguing with Moses.
Why are we going this way? You brought us all the way out here just to die of hunger?

If only we'd stayed the Pharaoh's slaves, we'd be eating our fill.

And they dreamed of the bread and meat they had eaten in Egypt.

But God heard them. And said unto Moses: Worry not. *At even, ye shall eat flesh,*
and in the morning ye shall be filled with bread.

That very evening, thousands of quail overwhelmed their camp.
They built fine fires and feasted on them, roasted.

The next morning, the desert sands were sparkling like silver.
The dew had covered the ground with fine, frost-like scales.

What on Earth is that? the people asked.

God, surprised that they didn't understand, said: *This is the bread which the LORD hath given you to eat.* Everyone can take each day what he needs, no more and no less.

And, of course, in a desert, you're thirsty. You brought us all the way out here just to die of thirst? Better a slave in Egypt than dead in a desert!

By now, Moses had had enough. The people were threatening to stone him.

But God heard them. And he said to Moses: No problem. Just knock on the rock at Horeb *and there shall come water out of it, that the people may drink.*

Arriving at the bottom of the Sinai, they made their camp.

Moses said to them: Help out! Take charge! I can't do it all myself.

And up the mountain went Moses to God.

God cried out from the night and the clouds: *Ye have seen what I did unto the Egyptians, and how I bare you on eagles' wings, and brought you unto myself.* Now listen up: If you keep my covenant, *then ye shall be a peculiar treasure unto me.*

God gave Moses ten commandments.
Ten commandments carved in stone.
Ten commandments for living as one.

1

I am Yhwh, your God. I delivered you
from Egypt and slavery.

2

Thou shalt have no other gods before me.
And thou shalt make no images of what is in
the sky, on the land, and in the waters.

3

Thou shalt not take the Lord's name in vain.

4

Thou shalt observe the Sabbath
and on that day, do no work.

5.

Thou shalt honor thy father and thy mother.

6.

Thou shalt not kill.

7.

Thou shalt not commit adultery.

8.

Thou shalt not steal.

9.

Thou shalt not bear false witness.

10.

Thou shalt not covet thy neighbor's wife nor anything belonging to him.

Lightning struck, and the mountain trembled and smoked.

And Moses drew near unto the thick darkness where God was.

And the people stood afar off.

17.

The Golden Calf

or The Invisible Led Astray

based on *The Book of Deuteronomy*, chapter 34

In which they prefer to worship what they can see rather than trust in the invisible. And we learn what happens to people who try to capture the divine ... in a calf.

The people walked three months through the desert to get to Mount Sinai.

On the mountain, God gave Moses the commandments of responsibility and freedom.

How to live in peace.

How to provide for all.

How to love and honor God.

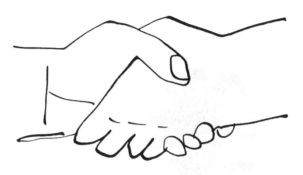

And how to love and honor others.

But it took a long time. A very long time
for Moses to come down from the mountain.

The people below grew restless and rebellious.
Where is Moses? What's he doing up there?

To calm them down, Aaron suggested that they take all the gold jewelry they owned and melt it down to make a statue . . .

The statue of a golden calf!

The image sparkled with all their hidden desires.

Finally, a reassuring representation of a god, the god of passions and possessions.

These be thy gods, O Israel! cried the people.
And they ate and drank and danced all night.

In the distance, the mountain trembled and smoked more and more.

God was furious. *For thou art a stiff-necked people . . .*

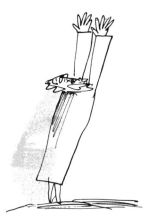

Moses begged God not to stop loving the people nor to give up his promise.

There will be as many children as stars in the sky.
And a land of milk and honey.

When he came down from the mountain, the angry Moses broke the tablets
on which the finger of God had written the commandments.

He stopped the dancing. And turned the golden calf to dust.
And mixed the dust with water and made the people drink.

And that night, in the camp, at Moses's command, three thousand men were killed.

Then Moses left the camp and pitched his tent outside.

And it was protected by the shadow of God.
Every night, a luminous pillar of cloud hovered over it.

Moses cut two new stone tablets just like the first.

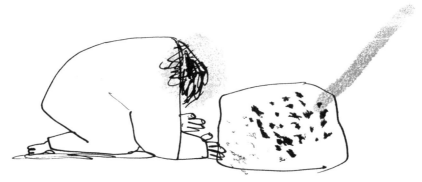

Up on the mountain, God again wrote in the stone
the ten commandments that he had spoken.

And told Moses how to build an ark to store the tablets
that constituted the covenant between him and his people.

The box was really a small house,
a portable temple that the people could keep always with them.

Everyone took part in the construction.
They brought wood and cloth, gold and silver, and sparkling gems.

Made of acacia and gold plated:
The Ark of the Covenant.

Moses was now very old.
At 120, he was having a little trouble getting around.

He asked Joshua to succeed him. From now on he would guide the people.

Moses knew that he would never reach the Promised Land.
But he kept the Covenant he had made with God.

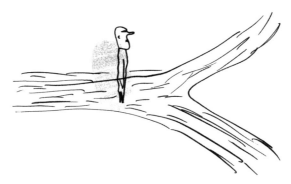

This Covenant made everyone responsible for all as well as for himself.
Now life and happiness or death and misery was each person's choice.

Leaving the Plain of Moab, Moses slowly climbed Mount Nebo.
Facing Jericho.

From the top, he saw the Promised Land stretching all the way to the sea.

And there he died, having written the law of God.

To this day, they've never found his grave.

18.

Jericho

or The Bloody Saga of Land Acquisition

based on *The Book of Joshua*, chapters 1 through 6

In which the Promised Land is conquered
by the intercession of a foreign woman,
a prostitute. And the invincible walls
crumble from the call of a trumpet.

Joshua repeated the teachings of Moses constantly under his breath.

How to get his people to the land of milk and honey?
How to get across the delta of the Jordan?

The plain was flooded. Everywhere was water.
The people waited on the banks of the overflowing river.

God would work miracles. Joshua just knew it.

The twelve tribes of Israel walked one after the other up the bank of the river
as the Ark of the Covenant was carried on ahead.
When the bearers stepped into the water, the river stopped.

And all the people crossed.

Each tribe took one stone from the riverbed.

And Joshua set up the twelve stones in the midst of Jordan,
and they are there unto this day. Standing witness.

With the walls of Jericho there in the distance.
A walled city. No one went in; no one came out.

Through the streets, two shadows flit. Spies sent by Joshua to look around a bit.

Near the ramparts lived a floozy named Rahab.
She had heard word of Moses and his God.

The spies, pursued by the men of the king of Jericho, knocked on her door, and she agreed to help.

She took them up onto the roof and hid them beneath her sheets.

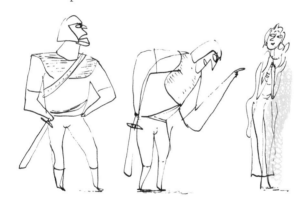

The king's men questioned her: Where are the spies?
They have gone with the night, she replied.

Then she let them down from the roof by a rope.

You've saved our lives, said the spies.

Thou shalt bind this line of scarlet thread in the window, and we'll save you in turn.

Back at camp, the people were getting anxious. Our courage is failing, they cried.

Then a strange horseman appeared to Joshua, saying:
As Commander of the army of the Lord I have now come. And you'll win.

The next day, the Hebrew warriors walked all around Jericho.
And again, once a day for six days.

Seven priests with seven rams' horn trumpets carried the Ark of the Covenant.

On the seventh day, they walked around the town seven times.
The priests sounded their trumpets.

Joshua commanded: *Shout, for the Lord has given you the city!*

And the walls of Jericho fell.

The warriors entered the city.
And massacred men, women, children, even the elderly and all the animals.

Only Rahab and her house were spared. A woman, both harlot and enemy, had helped Israel.

The city was in ashes.

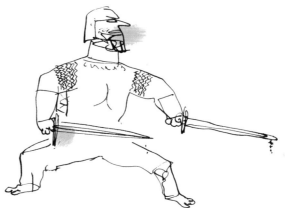

It was the first of many conquests. God had made his people victorious.

All the enemy kings were hanged from a tree.

And God unleashed a hail of stones.

And cut the tendons of all the horses.

And Joshua stopped the sun.

Neither it nor the moon moved again until the massacre was done.

One by one, every city was besieged, conquered, and destroyed:
Makkedah, Lachish, Libna, Eglon, Hebron, Debir, Kadesh, Gaza, Goshen, Gibeon . . .

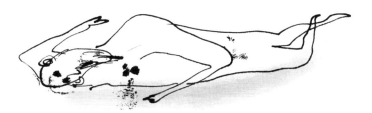

They ran a sword through everything alive.
From the plain to the mountain, nothing survived.

Then the land rested from war.

Canaan was divided among among the twelve victorious tribes.

Joshua had grown old, still repeating Moses's teachings.

He said to the gathered people: *Behold, this day I am going the way of all the Earth.*
But never forget that God gave you victory.

19.

Ruth

or The Enchanted Harvest

based on *The Book of Ruth*

In which a young Moabite stranger chooses
Israel from love and gleans the heart of Boaz,
becoming the great-great-grandmother of
King David.

I'm going to tell you a tale from ancient times, when the judges ruled Israel.

The story of Ruth, a young foreign woman who'd lost everything—husband, protection . . . and yet she hung on until she finally found happiness under the wing of the God of Israel.

The story begins in Bethlehem, "the house of bread," the city in which King David would live. But that year, there was no bread left.

Struck by the famine, gentle Naomi, her husband, Elimelech, and their two sons fled.

They migrated north to foreign lands.

Exhausted, Elimelech soon died.

Everyone cried.

After a while, the two sons took two beautiful women from the region, Orpah and Ruth, as wives.

Ten years passed. On the great plain of Moab, north of the Dead Sea,

three small, dark silhouettes headed toward Bethlehem.

One old woman, empty and sad. That's Naomi. And two young women in mourning for their husbands, who'd died. Orpah and Ruth.

We must part, said Naomi. I'm too old. I'm going back to Bethlehem.

Everyone cried. And Orpah went back to Moab.

But not Ruth. She stayed with Naomi. *For wither thou goest, I will go.*

Thy people shall be my people. Your nights, my own. And your grave, as well.

In Bethlehem, all rejoiced. Naomi had returned!

Call me not Naomi, nor my gentle one, but say instead Mara, as bitter I've become.
I return ruined.

In Bethlehem, it was time to reap.

Ruth needed work, and so went to the fields to glean.

The powerful Boaz, a wealthy landowner and Naomi's distant relation, noticed her.

He asked the harvesters: *Whose damsel is this?*

She's a poor foreigner, but a hard worker. She asked permission to glean the fields after us.

Boaz was moved.
This young foreigner had put herself under the protection of the God of Israel.

He gave her permission to come as often as she liked and gave her something to drink and eat.

Every night, Ruth gave Naomi everything she'd gleaned.

Boaz is my only remaining relation, Naomi told her. And you need a protector.
Wash thyself therefore, and anoint thee.

And put thy raiment upon thee. And lie down next to Boaz as he sleeps.

At night, Boaz slept among his harvest.
Ruth found him and lay down next to him beneath the moon.

[p295]

In the middle of the night, he woke up from the cold, and there she was.

It's me, Ruth, she said. I'm yours. Please take me under your wing.

Again, Boaz was moved.

The next day, Boaz sat down at the gate of the city and made a deal.
He bought all the land that had belonged to Naomi's husband and took Ruth as his wife.

They had one child, Obed.

Old Naomi took the child in her arms.
He became the father of Jesse, who became in turn the father of the great king David.

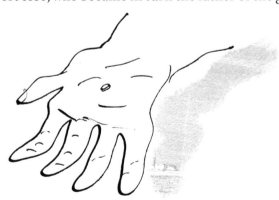

An old story, tiny as a kernel of wheat, thus became one of the greatest stories of an entire people.

20.

Samson and Delilah

or The Indomitable Judge

based on *The Book of Judges*, chapters 14 through 16

In which we learn that one must not play
upon the nerves of heroes. And how a
weakness for women can lead to ruin, helped
along by some underhanded dealings.

And it came to pass that there was neither king nor temple.
The Philistines ruled over the people of Israel.

And the people of Israel waited for someone to free them.

A barren woman was given a promise.

An angel of God told her: *Thou shalt conceive and bear a son.*
And he shall begin to deliver Israel out of the hand of the Philistines.

The child was born, and they called him Samson.

He wore his hair long and never had it cut, a sign that he was promised to God.

People soon noticed that he was unusually strong.

A lion attacked him, and the lion lost.
Defeated as easily as might have been a goat.

Attacked by thirty men, he didn't turn a hair, but massacred them all in one fell swoop.

The people of Israel cheered: What a hero!

But like all heroes, Samson had a weakness.

He was a lover. He loved women.
He met a pretty, young Philistine and threw all caution to the wind.

He fell under her spell and made her his wife. *Fait accompli.*

And the Philistines didn't like it one bit. They burned her alive, along with her father.

The hero was furious.

So Samson trapped three hundred foxes. And tied them together with a torch at each tail.
And let them lose in the Philistines' fields.
Their crops went up in flames.

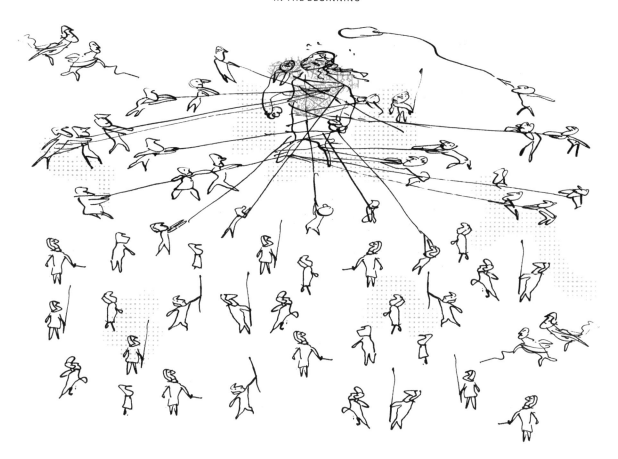

The Philistines sent three thousand men to capture Samson and tie him down.

But the giant simply burst the bonds.

And wiped out the Philistines with the jawbone of an ass.

In Gaza, he rested.
Spending the night with a particularly cute prostitute.

They took advantage of it to imprison him in the city.

But Samson simply tore off the city gate and carried it away.

And then one day, he fell in love with Delilah. Dark, beautiful, and poor.

Every night Delilah badgered him, trying to get him to reveal the secret of his strength.

Samson refused to comment. *How canst thou say, I love thee?* she demanded.

And she, in turn, refused his advances. Finally, he gave in.

His strength was all in his hair, he said.

So Delilah waited until Samson was asleep

and then shaved his head.

At last the Philistines could capture God's giant without resistance.

They gouged out his eyes. He would never again see the sun—nor women.

They threw him in prison.

Hero demoted. Giant cut down. They mocked him.

But his hair grew back . . .

One day he asked: Let me out to lean against that column.

And with all his force returned, he knocked the column down and the whole building toppled.
We'll all die together! he cried.
And so he died of his own strength, and killed more men with his death than he'd killed
in his whole life. Strong yet vulnerable, Samson preferred destruction to shame.

21.

Samuel and Saul

or The Coronation of the First King

based on *The First Book of Samuel*, chapters 3 through 16

In which Israel finds a king,
though it's quite a trial.
And Saul ends tragically,
despite his victories in battle.

And it came to pass that Israel had no king.

There was a boy, Samuel. His mother, Hannah, had prayed for a son.

Every year Hannah made him a new little coat.

The young Samuel grew.
Under Eli, the priest, he served the God that rules over life and death.

One night, a voice called out to him. Once, twice . . .
He went into Eli, who said: *I called not; lie down again.*
The third time, Eli got it: It was God who was calling him.

As Samuel got older, he became a seer. A prophet.

It was an era in which the people were sad and afraid of one another.

They began to demand a king: We want to be like other people. We want a king.
Samuel said to them: But a king will take your sons and make them soldiers or peasants
and will take your daughters and make them serve him. You'll be the slaves of a tyrant!

You're too old to help us. Give us a king!

Samuel was discouraged. But God told him: *A man will come to you.*
And thou shalt anoint him to be captain over my people Israel.

A poor man had a young and beautiful son. He was Saul.

One day, Saul was out looking for his father's lost horses.
Could not find them anywhere. So he went to ask Samuel, the seer.

Samuel received him like a prince.
They partied all night.

Just as day was dawning, Samuel took Saul up to the roof.
And anointed him with oil and said: Over Israel you shall rule.

Samuel had recognized the king.

But I'm so small, thought Saul.

Samuel called all the families of all the people together.
And said: His name is Saul.

He was hiding behind some boxes. They brought him out—and he was strong and tall.

God save the king! the people shouted.

King Saul fought all the enemies of Israel.
His life was nothing but battle and slaughter—rather depressing.

God asked Saul to wipe out the ancient enemy, the Amalekites.

Utterly destroy all that they have . . . slay both man and woman, infant and suckling, ox and sheep, camel and ass. Wipe them off the face of the Earth. And you will erase your own memories of violence and hate.

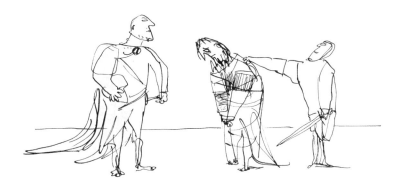

But though Saul's victorious army took plunder and prisoners, Saul spared the enemy king.

Samuel was furious! Saul had not obeyed God's word.

Samuel executed the Amalek king. And abandoned Saul, who never saw him again.

But as he turned to go, Saul grabbed him by his coat, which rent in two.
Just as, said Samuel, *the Lord hath rent the kingdom of Israel from thee this day.*

See Saul: infinitely sad. And no longer king.

His sadness grew and gnawed at him, gnawing too at the protective shadow of God.
The sad giant was left with nothing but darkness and ghosts.

The music of a young shepherd, David, was his only consolation.
And Saul, in his distress, became very fond of David.

22.

David and Goliath

or The Rebellious Child

based on *The First Book of Samuel*, chapter 17

In which a mere child slays a giant
and a shepherd playing a harp offers
solace to Saul in his sadness. Before
becoming a victorious military leader.

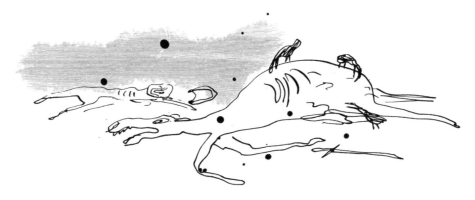

In the Israel of King Saul's day, war was all the rage.
Battle after battle.

The Philistines on one hill, the Israelites on the other.
And between them, a river of blood.

How to stop the carnage?

The enemy's cast of thousands included a giant nine feet tall,
with armor of bronze and iron, and armed to the teeth.

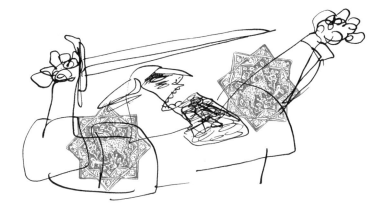

He taunted the Israeli soldiers: *Why are ye come out to set your battle in array?*

Slaves of Saul, here's my deal:

Choose a single man and send him out to fight me.

Whoever wins, wins for all.

Panic in the Israeli camp. Goliath! Who could possibly stand up to him?

Rumor ran that Saul would make anyone who killed Goliath fabulously rich and give him his own daughter for a wife.

Young David, local musician and shepherd *par excellence*, pricked up his ears.

You wimp! his brothers teased, be content with simply watching the war.

To cheer himself up, Saul liked to listen to David on his harp.

Which gave David the opportunity to say: *Thy servant will go and fight with this Philistine.*

Ah! But next to Goliath, you're but a child, Saul replied.
But thanks anyway.

Ah! said David in return: I've fought wild beasts when they attacked my sheep.

I snatched a little lamb right out of the mouth of one.
God has saved me from the claws of lions and bears. He'll extend the favor as far as Goliath.

So Saul dressed David for battle. Bronze breast plate and helmet.

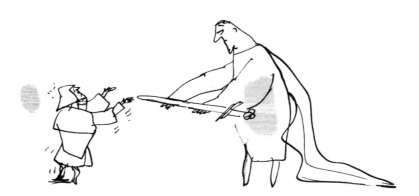

And the royal sword.

But the rather frail David couldn't even walk under all that weight.

So he popped back into his shepherd's cloak,

and chose from the river five good stones.

And walked up to Goliath with only a slingshot. You wimp! said the giant.
I will give thy flesh unto the fowls of the air, and to the beasts of the field.

Not so fast, said David, *for I come to thee in the name of the Lord of hosts.*
I'm going to kill you and chop off your head.

Furious, Goliath bore down upon David, who got him right between the eyes
with the very first stone. Done. See Goliath, now historic.

David leapt upon him and, as promised, off went his head.

The Philistines were shocked, to say the least.

While back in Jerusalem, David gave Saul Goliath's head on a platter.
He was made the top military leader, and on he went, from victory to victory.

And after each victory, the women danced and sang:
Saul hath slain his thousands, and David his ten thousands.

Which made Saul furious
and drove him rather mad.

One evening, as David was playing his harp,
Saul drew his sword and cried: *I will smite David even to the wall with it.*

But David dodged him. He didn't want to hurt the king.

Which made Saul realize that God was with David. Which frightened him.
He became more and more somber, and David, more and more famous.

23.

David and Bathsheba

or Crime, Punishment, and Absolution

based on *The Second Book of Samuel*, chapter 11

In which David becomes a great king
and faces the consequences of ravishing
Bathsheba, the wife of his greatest warrior.

In King Saul's day, it was the sword that reigned.
Leaving behind but bitterness and grief.

Battle. Slaughter.

The King was so vicious that even David feared for his life.

Until one night, a warrior—his armor in tatters, his head covered in ashes—
brought David the crown of King Saul.

Mortally wounded, Saul had asked to be succeeded by the one he most hated.

David cried and grieved.

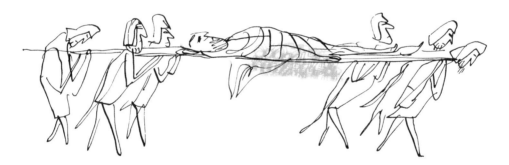

How can heroes be slain in battle?
Why do we kill each other, only to cry over it later?

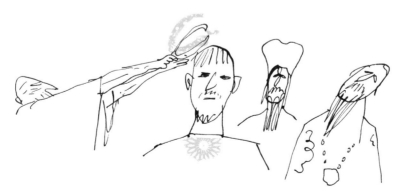

So David became king, but the tribes of Israel kept on fighting.

Abner killed Asahel, Joab's brother. Joab killed Abner. Amnon, Absalom's brother
and the son of David, raped their sister Tamar. Absalom killed his brother.
Absalom raped his father David's wives. Joab, the head of David's army, killed Absalom.

And threw his bloody body into a pit in the woods.

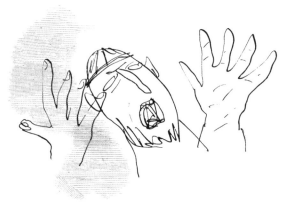

David cried out: *O my son Absalom, O Absalom, my son, my son!*

Then he locked himself away in his palace in Jerusalem. Overcome with grief, unable to sleep.

All night long, he walked along the terrace, casting his eye across the great city.

Where he spied a woman taking her bath. Very young. And very beautiful to look upon.

It was Bathsheba, the wife of Uriah the Hittite, one of his most faithful men.

David was a great fan of the women of Jerusalem. He had Bathsheba brought to him.

And slept with her. Bathsheba kept mum.

When David learned that Bathsheba was pregnant, he told Joab to bring Uriah back from the front.

Uriah came back to Jerusalem.

Relax, said David, trying to get him drunk, and above all, go and take pleasure with your wife.

But Uriah had an exceptionally loyal streak and was determined to return to his men.
They were right in the middle of a war—he couldn't just abandon them!

So David asked Uriah to deliver a letter to Joab at the front.

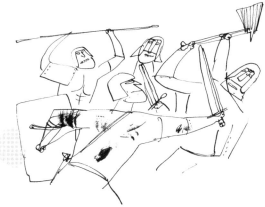

Little did Uriah know that the letter said:
Set ye Uriah in the forefront of the hottest battle that he may be smitten, and die.

Which was done.
Blood ran. Warriors wailed.

And David took care of Bathsheba, the wife of his most loyal soldier—
a man he had killed rather than be forced to admit to his own treachery.

The prophet Nathan: *furious*. And so God took the life of
David and Bathsheba's first son but spared that of their second, Solomon.

And before he knew it, King David grew old. And cold.
Who could succeed him in his deepening evening?

Nathan and Bathsheba reminded David of his promise: My son Solomon will reign after me.

Thus the promise of God survived murder, lies, and adultery.

24.

Elijah at Horeb
or The Almost-Silence of God

based on *The First Book of Kings*, chapters 17 through 19

In which it appears that carrying God's word
is not an easy job. And Elijah in his despair is
led to understand that God, at the time,
spoke in the sound of his silence.

And it came to pass that an odd little person, a stranger and foreigner,
came to tell Ahab, the fearsome king of Israel:

There shall not be dew nor rain these years, but according to my word.

He was Elijah. No one knew where he came from.

The sky dried up.
Drought. Famine.

336

The furious king threatened him. So Elijah slipped away.

When he popped up again one day, completely unexpected, Ahab cried:
You! What are you doing here?! You troublemaker!

And Elijah replied: Not I, but you and your queen Jezebel—
you're the ones making all the trouble by following Baal instead of the God of Israel.

Elijah, alone, defied the prophets of Baal, all 450 of them.

A huge crowd watched from the top of Mount Carmel.

Call ye on the name of your gods, and I will call on the name of the Lord.
The one who first lights the sacrificial fires wins.

The prophets of Baal started off.

They danced and prayed and beat themselves. But nothing.
No fire. No flames. No god.

Then it was Elijah's turn. He walked up.

And called out to Yhwh, his God.

And a great fire flared up, wiping out everything in its path.

The victorious Elijah slit the throats of all the prophets of Baal.

And at last upon the kingdom, rain fell.

But the jealous Jezebel wanted him killed, so once again he slipped away,

heading off across the desert, alone.

Exhausted hero. Distraught prophet.

Finally, he collapsed under a tree. Enough! he said. I'd rather die.
Why survive? I can't do anything right.

Elijah fell asleep.

An angel woke him up. Eat, drink, and get on with it, he said.

Elijah set off again, going the way Moses had gone. Through the desert, forty days and forty nights.

But once arrived at the mountain of Horeb, where God had appeared to Moses, he found no one.

Suddenly, a voice: *What doest thou here, Elijah?* Elijah replied, I'm alone.
I'm the only one left to defend the love of God; everyone else wants Baal.

And the voice said, God will come.

But God didn't come and didn't reply, as he had done in earlier times.

Nothing from the wind off the mountains.

Nothing from the Earth, furiously trembling.

Nothing from the fire.

No; God came in the sound of silence. A sound as soft as dust.

And in his loneliness, Elijah understood: The living God is now the God of the silent and the soft.

Now to Israel, Elijah could return.

And to the sky, where he later disappeared.

And from then on, we never close the door, but wait for him,

Always saving him a chair.

25.

Solomon and the Queen of Sheba

or Wisdom and the Evening of a King

based on *The First Book of Kings*, chapters 5 through 11, and 18 and 19

In which, among other marvels, a foreign
queen and her court come to consult Wisdom
in person. She is amazed by all Solomon says,
even though he is weak with age.

Solomon, the king of Israel, had given his whole heart to wisdom.
The wisdom that existed before history even started.

He dreamed big and got very rich.

He began by honoring the promise of his father, David,
and in Jerusalem built a great temple to Yhwh.

From Lebanon, he brought whole forests of cypress and cedar. For seven years they labored.

And God said to Solomon: *I have heard thy prayer and I have hallowed this house, and mine eyes and mine heart shall be there perpetually.*

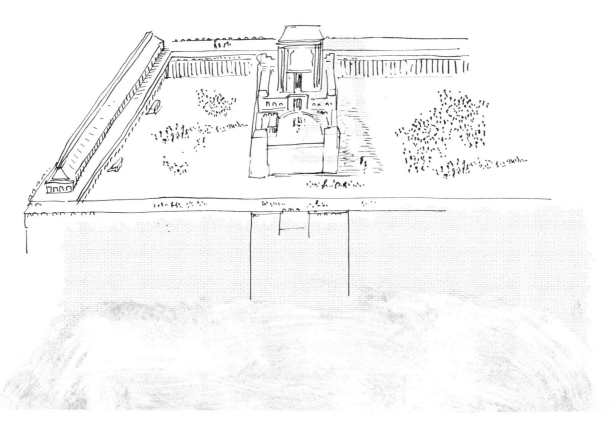

The beauty of the Temple was proof of eternal wisdom.

And God said yes, he would live there among men.

But, Solomon asked, how can God be contained in a temple
if the sky and the sky of the sky are not large enough to hold him?

Suddenly the Temple was wrapped in a thick fog.
The priests could no longer pray.

God said to Solomon, I have heard you.

And I will be there in that house with my name.
And there with my eyes will be the beauty of the world.
And its wisdom, there with my heart.

But if ye shall at all turn from me, or from my eyes, or from my heart, I'll wipe Israel right off the map. And the entire world will mock you before the ruins of your temple.

Solomon was deeply moved.
God had agreed to hear the prayers of anyone who came to him in this house!

All throughout Jerusalem, they held huge feasts.
In two weeks, they sacrificed 22,000 cattle and 120,000 sheep!

Wisdom came to live in Solomon's heart.

And the news of it spread around the world.

One evening, there came into Jerusalem a queen, having traveled from foreign lands far to the south.
Her journey had been long.

It was for wisdom that she had come.

She was the most beautiful of queens.

And she came bearing lavish gifts and creatures they had never seen.
Solomon greeted the new animals one by one.

And then listened to the questions of the queen. She wanted to see everything,
to learn everything, and to share everything. Down to her very own heart.

Solomon knew all the answers.
The Queen of Sheba was amazed by his wisdom.

And it came to pass that Solomon grew lonely in his palace.
And asked himself: What good is it being wise?

As he got older, his mind began to wander.
He'd given his heart for wisdom and now found himself going mad.

Every night he lost himself among dozens of foreign women.
He had 300 concubines and 700 wives.

They drew him to their ways. They prayed to other gods.
Solomon went as far as to build them temples for their idols.

Which enraged the God of Israel.

Thou hast not kept my covenant, which I have commanded; I will surely rend the kingdom from thee.
And raze the Temple which rests not in your heart.

Lamentation far and wide. Woe to the country whose king has become a child.
From that day on, an evening shadow lay long over Israel.

26.

Love Scenes

or Love as Strong as Death

based on *The Song of Songs*

In which the great king Solomon of Jerusalem reveals many, many enigmas, but finds that of love the strangest by far. And true wisdom is earned by a song of love.

PROLOGUE — IN SOLOMON'S HAREM, JERUSALEM, THE PALACE OF THE KING.

In Jerusalem, Solomon, the son of David, was king.

So wise was he that he knew the language of the birds and the trees.

He was the happiest man in town.

He loved solving mysteries and was working on that of love.

But that didn't stop love from being love.

And Solomon the Sage was in love with love.

Among the women that Solomon loved, one surpassed all the rest.

Some called her the Shulamite, she who gives peace.

Others Susanna, because her beauty rivaled the lily and the rose.

The king brought her into his chamber.

ACT 1—THE DREAM. NIGHT IN THE CITY.

She thought of nothing but the kisses of her lover.

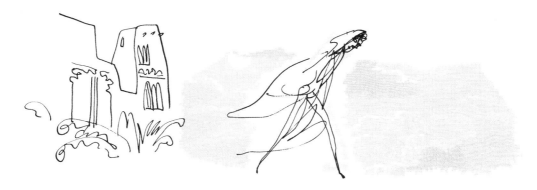

In the dark of night, she slipped out, unseen.

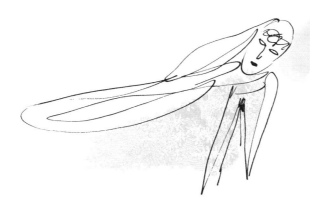

Guided alone by the light that lit her heart.

Shouvi, shouvi, ha-Shoulammit, shouvi, shouvi. Return, return, O Shulamite; return!

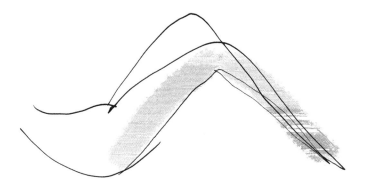

Your womb is an armful of wheat.

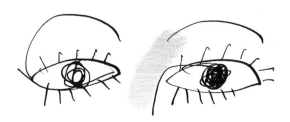

Your eyes two doves.

Your breasts twin fawns.

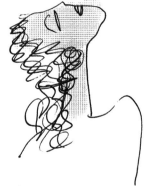

Dark, so gorgeously dark.
And much more beautiful than the daughters of Jerusalem.

She sings.

I sleep but my heart keeps watch.

It's love.
All young women love love.

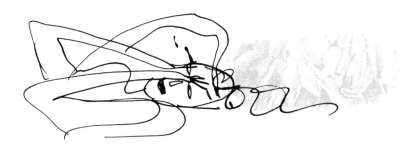

I'm sick with love.

Give me back my magic. With apples. And raisins.

Gazelles and hinds of the fields. Daughters of Jerusalem.

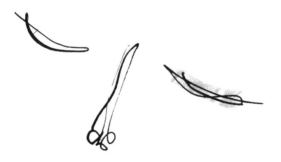

I beg you: Let love not wake up.

ACT 2—FLIGHT AND PURSUIT IN THE NIGHT. THE CITY. THE RAMPARTS.

Night after night, I seek the one I love.

I look for him in my bed. I look for him in the streets.

No luck. But the guards found me.
Stripped me of my cloak and struck me down.

Have you seen the one I love?

ACT 3—CONFRONTATION WITH SOLOMON. THE PALACE. KING'S COURT WITH GUARDS.

Solomon's cortege: Sixty terrible warriors, each striding through the night with a sword at his side.

Solomon asks: You, most beautiful of women, what is your secret?
Why is your love so different?

The response: My love is mine and his am I.

ACT 4—THE LOVER APPEARS. A DREAM? THE HILLS OF JERUSALEM.

And look now. My love who comes.

Before the morning breeze, before the shadows flee.

With a single leap over the hills. A stag. A small deer.

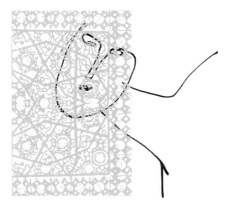

See him within our walls. At the window, he calls.

Let me see your face, he pleads.

My sister, my love, open to me.

She: I rise to open to my love.

I cast off my robe.
I hold out my hand. I tremble at the thought of him.

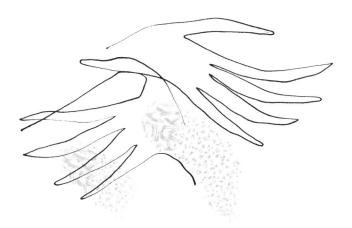

From my fingers drips the myrrh.

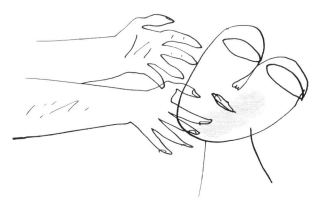

He: My love, here.
More beautiful than love.

As beautiful as Jerusalem.
Your hair is as a flock of goats unfurling down the hill.
Your cheek, half a pomegranate uncurled.

ACT 5—THE LOVERS DISAPPEAR. VINEYARDS AND ORCHARDS.

Return, O Shulamite; return! that we may look upon thee.

King Solomon is out in his vineyards.

These vines are mine and I am among them.

I live within the garden.

I will find you again, my love.

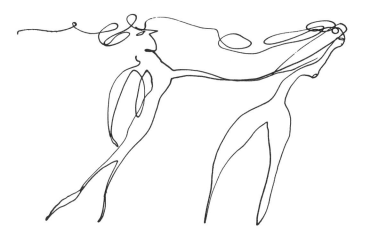

I will take you to my mother's house.

And beneath the tree, I will wake you up.

And place myself like a seal on your heart.

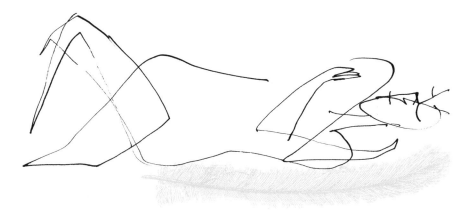

Love is as strong as death.

No river will carry it away.

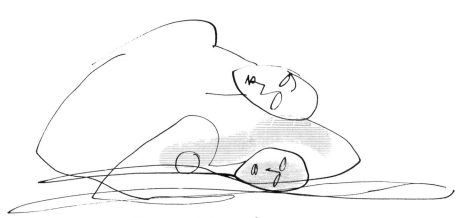

You cannot stay, my love.

Small deer over the mountains.

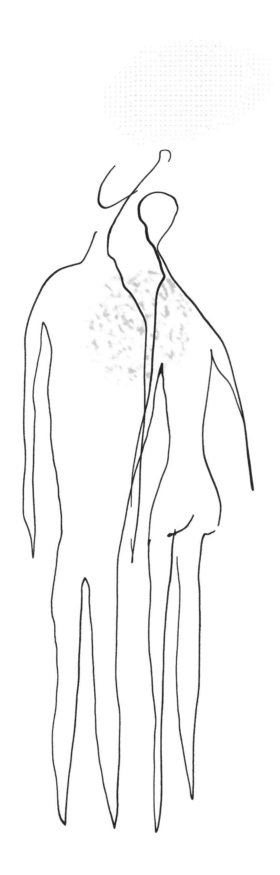

Love is as strong as death.

27.

Isaiah's Visions

or A Mysterious Liberator

based on *The Book of Isaiah*

In which we learn of the events that followed the catastrophe of exile. And a prophet who sees what no one else wants to see makes some alarming suggestions that no one wants to hear.

In the Temple of Jerusalem, King Hezekiah was wringing his hands in despair.

The armies of the terrible king of Assyria were threatening Jerusalem and Samaria.

The people were asking why their God-given kings couldn't protect them.

Kings will die, and kingdoms can be razed. The voice of Yhwh seemed very far away!
They turned to magicians and sorcerers because they were afraid.

But the voice of the prophet Isaiah rose in the Temple, saying: I have seen!

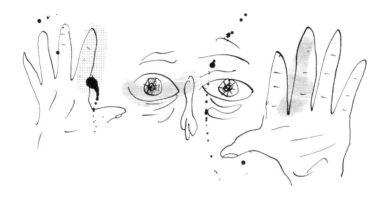

Isaiah saw what the others would not see. He became God's mouth and transmitted his speech.

And the great king of Assyria destroyed Samaria and the northern kingdom.
Exile and deportation. The refugees all fled to Jerusalem.

Fortresses toppled. Castles in ruin. Only Jerusalem still stood.

Left as a cottage in a vineyard! cried Isaiah.

Darkness and distress

as Yhwh said: *Shall I not, as I have done unto Samaria and her idols, so do to Jerusalem and her idols?*

Your sacrifices make me ill. The blood of lambs and bulls.

Your feasts and your prayer wheels. Blood and incense on your hands.

Friends tearing each other limb from limb.

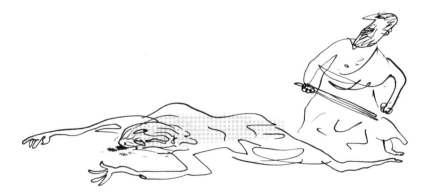

The young preying on the old.

You're all completely out of whack! Go back to being just.
Defend the widow and the orphan. The weak and the oppressed.

Without justice and the law, humanity will end.

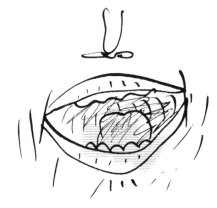

But with them, Jerusalem will be saved. Obey.

But everyone wondered:
Who will come to blow on the embers of this promise?

Isaiah repeated: A flame is stirring. Hope is rising.
Your wrongs, red as blood, will be bleached white as snow.

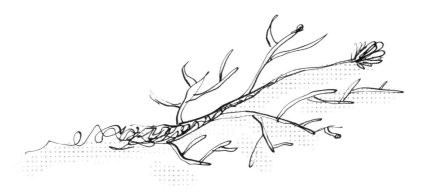

No, all is not night; the branch will flower again.

A king will come. A woman will give birth to someone who will save us,
and will treat the weak with justice.

And defeat the mean and raise up the downtrodden.

The wolf also shall dwell with the lamb,

and the lion purr,

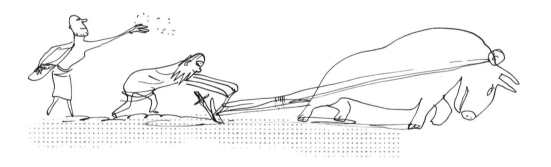

and ploughshares be made from our swords.

But king after king refused to hear these words.

Isaiah died, but his voice did not. It said: Stop holding on to the past.
God will make a new sky, a new land.

In the year 586 BCE Jerusalem was captured

and the Temple destroyed, the king dethroned,

and many sent into exile in Babylon.

Throughout the ruins, Isaiah's voice resounded.

Your liberator is coming. The king for whom you wait—though you'll never recognize him.
He's a nobody, a man without station. No stature, no beauty.

Barely human. Under suspicion and in considerable pain. He will carry your sufferings for you.

Welcome him; he will astound you.
Rejoice; you will come to believe the unbelievable.

28.

Ezekiel's Visions

or The Speech of One Mad-with-God

based on *The Book of Ezekiel*

In which a small man is exiled, his suitcase at his side. And goes on to describe terrifying visions of Jerusalem, which he thinks has prostituted itself.

For five years, the king of Judah and his court lived in exile on the banks of the river in Babylon.

One day a strange little man carrying a suitcase appeared among them.

It was Ezekiel.

God had possessed him, he said, in order to move through time and space.

A voice had told him: *Son of man, stand upon thy feet* and be on your way.

In the darkness of exile, he had visions that amazed him.

And made him denounce violence, terrorism, luxury, and injustice.

He saw the heavens open and divine power reveal itself like a great fire in the sky.

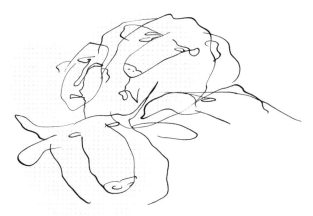

Out of the midst thereof came the likeness of four living creatures
each with four heads: a man, a lion, an eagle, and an ox.

And four wheels of fire.

Stand! the voice commanded . . .

and behold, an hand was sent unto me; and, lo, a roll of a book therein
and in it written: lamentations, mourning, woe.

Ezekiel had to eat this book. But despair turned to honey in his mouth.

One night he learned that his cherished wife had died.
In silence, he sighed, but did not put on mourning.

Everyone was scandalized. Ezekiel replied: It's a sign from God.

Why wear mourning for your lost illusions?

He drew a map of Jerusalem on a tile.
With an assault tower, war machines, and an army laying siege.

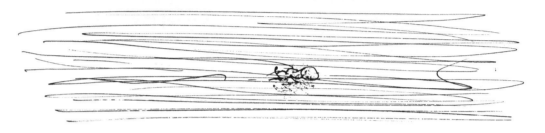

Look, that's Jerusalem, he said.
A little naked girl out in a field, abandoned at birth.
Bathing in her own blood.

Only God noticed her. He picked her up and washed her clean.

Jerusalem grew.
She became beautiful: shapely breasts, long, flowing hair. Embroidered robes, leather sandals, jewels.

God took her under his wing.

He swore an alliance.

But Jerusalem flaunted her beauty and idolized her jewels.

She became the whore of Egypt, of Ashur.

On the ramparts, she spread her legs.

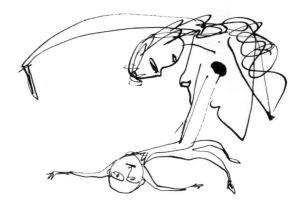

She butchered her children and sacrificed them to idols.

The exiles understood: Our hopes are dashed. Our bones are dead. We're done for.

But no, for neither despair nor death is the end.

For he who believes in forgiveness, history is never over.

The ruined cities will thrive once again.

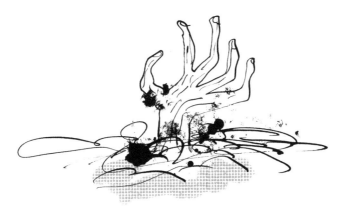

A voice said: I will raise you from your graves. I will bring you back to your land.

No more idols, no more insurrections, but a pact of peace.

By my forgiveness, you will know that I am Yhwh.

And a great wind carried Ezekiel to a valley full of bones in the blazing sun.

Ezekiel said to them: Listen to the word of Yhwh; listen to him.

A breath passed over the dead and the slain.
And with a terrible din, the bones came back together again.

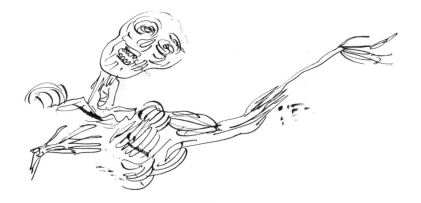

The flesh regrew, and the bones took on muscle and skin.

Ezekiel was then taken to see the Temple rebuilt along with the entire city and its twelve new gates. A perfect city in every way.

Hope gives us wings. God gives us new lands where peace and justice reign.

All of God's creation will never fear again.

29.

Jonah

or The Sadness of a Minor Prophet

based on *The Book of Jonah*

In which we learn what happens when you think of nothing but your own pain. And Jonah, thinking he's escaping his destiny, fulfills it in spite of himself and manages to save his worst enemies from God's wrath.

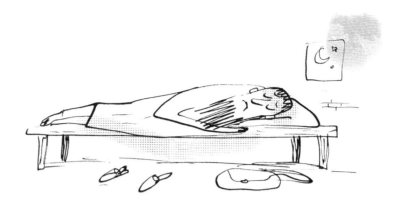

Jonah slept. He was sad.

Then a voice said: *Arise, go to Nineveh, that great city, and cry against it.*

So Jonah got up.

To the east: Nineveh, capital of the enemies of Israel.
To the west: Tarshish, the distance.

I think I'll head west, Jonah said to himself. Not to Nineveh. And why me, anyway?
They're our enemies; what could I possibly have to say?

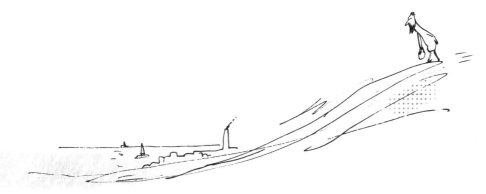

He didn't want to offend God. But he didn't want to have to face him either.
So he went down to the sea to leave.

At the port he found a boat, paid his fare, and got on board.

A great storm arose.

The sailors were frightened. They threw everything they could spare overboard
and began calling on their gods.

Jonah decided to sleep it off, and went down into the ship.

The captain shook him awake: *What meanest thou, O sleeper?*
Arise, call upon thy God!

The sailors drew lots to see who was at fault. The lot fell to Jonah.

They began to ask him questions.

And he replied: I'm a Hebrew. My God created the world.

But the sailors were worried: What should they do with him?

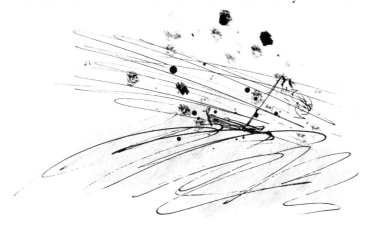

The storm grew worse.

Johan suggested: Since it's my fault, throw me into the sea.

The sailors called on Jonah's God: Stop us from killing this man!

No response.

So they threw him overboard.

And a huge and terrible fish swallowed him whole.

And the storm calmed down.

For three nights in the belly of the fish, Jonah languished, bemoaning.

All around him, nothing but the dark.

He felt like he'd been thrown down a well.

Or locked up in a cell.

He knew he had to get through the black night of his misery.

And in that darkness, he called out to Yhwh.

My life is a wreck, but I remember you, my God.

He wanted out of the well, out of the night.

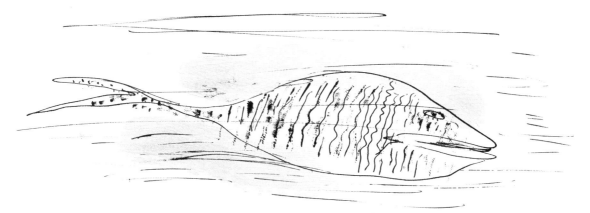

But how to say the unsayable? And free oneself from the mortal coil?

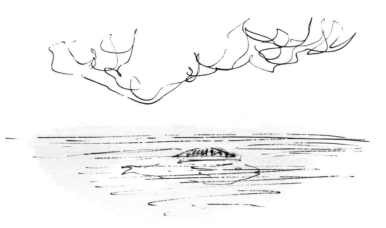

Yhwh heard, and had a word with the fish,

who tossed Jonah out onto the sand.

Where he heard the voice again: *Arise, go to Nineveh, that great city*
and say what I tell you to say.

Jonah walked for three days.

And then announced to Nineveh that it would be leveled forty days later.

To his surprise, they actually listened.

The whole city fasted and asked forgiveness.

The king of Nineveh, sitting on a pile of ashes, ordered everyone—
man, woman, child, and beast—to dress up in sackcloth.

And put an end to the violence. And so Yhwh reconsidered his decision.

Jonah was furious: Telling evil people that they're going to the devil was fine,
but he couldn't quite handle the thought of a pardon.

He'd rather die.

So he went away.

One night, God grew him a small tree for shelter.

Jonah was happy—finally alone and in the shade. And not worried about others' fate.

But there was a worm in the tree, and the tree died.

The sun beat down on Jonah's head.

He collapsed.

He wanted to die.
Why did you kill my tree? he cried.

And God replied: Your anger is distorting your perspective.
What is a small tree that grew in a single night compared to an entire city that repents—

thousands of people who may not even know their right from their left?

Why allow endless darkness to defeat forgiveness?

30.

A Psalm

or The Song of a Survivor

based on *The Book of Psalms*

In which hope returns in the voice of a small, fierce person lost in the dark and searching for the meaning and memory of God the Savior.

When all is lost, what remains?

I think of days long past. When Jerusalem had a king.

What changed?

I'm just a small man cowering in the dark. Abandoned for good.

I cry out.

Gone is God's love.
Gone is his word.

I remember past wonders, things God did for our fathers.

I remember the music at night.
And I sing the songs of sad king Saul, like David once sang.

But do the shadows rise to sing of God?

I have more enemies than hairs on my head.

I can't sleep—I stare into the night like an owl in a tree.

All alone at so sad a moment.

Why have you forsaken me?

I am mocked by all.

I am water, lost in its flow.

Scattered bones.

Shard of clay.

Dogs' prey.

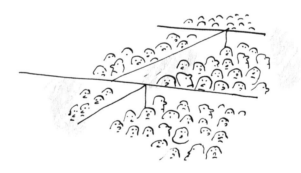

How empty is man! Trapped like a steer sent for slaughter.

Yes—what is man that you should remember him?

Your foes flee. You scatter kings.

In the dark, I consider your marvels. You, my shepherd.

Man in his splendor simply does not get it. He dies like a dog.

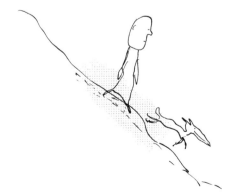

Whereas you know everything. My path. My thoughts.

If I climb to the sky, you are there. If I lie among the dead, there you are.

With you, shadows have no shadows. Night mirrors day.

You weave the sky with bare hands. And ply it with moon and stars.

And me—you've made almost a god of me. You've put everything at my feet.

Sheep, cattle, the beasts of the field. Fish and birds.

And have tied me to my mother, heart to heart.

I'm a marvel. Amazing.

You know each of my bones: Though I was made in secret, you knew me before I was born.

My foes, you know. My heart, you've read. You watch over me so I don't take the wrong road.

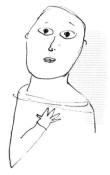

I am with you when I awake.
To me you speak, and your words scar my heart.

From the heights, you hold out your hand. Pluck me from the watery abyss. Deliver me from evil men.

Toward the mountains, I raise my eyes.
I am a bird escaping the hunter's net.

And I cry out with everyone else:

Hallelujah!

Hail! Love Yhwh! Hail You—yeah!

31.

Job

or The Scandal of Innocence

based on *The Book of Job*

In which we find, behind the terrible injustice of suffering, a very old legend and what was said about it, as well as about the mysterious character who, despite everything, managed to negotiate the nightmare of his existence.

Since the fall of the kingdom of Judah, the Earth had become a stranger.

We wondered: If God, who is good, made all, why is there wrong?

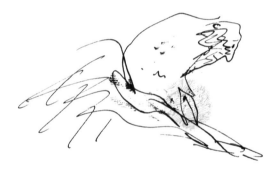

We're like Job, covered with ulcers on his pile of dung.

Job was a good man.

Rich and happy with seven sons, three daughters, and thousands of animals—
Mr. Big Shot, and loved by all.

And it came to pass that among men a strange man wandered,
spreading suspicion and doubt: the Negater!

He prowled around Job and his family.

He went to the court of Yhwh.

Ah! But Job doesn't love God for nothing, he claimed.

He has everything. He's covered. He's got it easy.

The Negater proposed an absurd bet: Put Job to the test.
Take everything from him and see if his love remains.

And so everything was taken away.

Fire from the sky destroyed his men, his goods, and his herds.
A desert wind destroyed the house where his children were dining, and they all died.

Job tore at his clothes.

Naked came I out of my mother's womb, and naked shall I return thither.
The Lord gave, and the Lord hath taken away.

Skin for skin, yea, said the Negater.

Job, from top to toe, was covered in sores.

He sat on a pile of ash and dung.

Three friends came by to console him. For seven days and seven nights, Job said not a word.

Then he spoke.

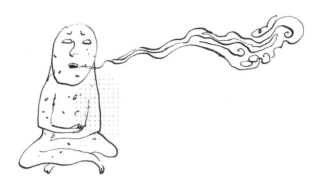

For among his misery, one treasure remained: his voice. He wanted to know what had gone wrong.

My days are troubled. My life is over.

His friends reproached him for complaining:
You talk too much, and it's not true. So much suffering accuses you.

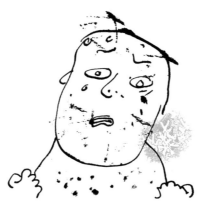

Friends of misery, Job replied, I will not hold my tongue.
Is it the suffering or the innocence that is the scandal?

Job no longer recognized the God he thought he knew.
He asked this terrible God a thing or two.

Why these dark and awful nights?
Why this spying on and policing men?

In defiance, Job wore his accusation like a crown.
And waited for God's reply.

He swore that somehow he would be saved.

And then declared: That's my last word. I have nothing more to say.

So now it was man against God.
Pain against Creation.

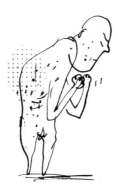

From within a whirlwind, twice God spoke.

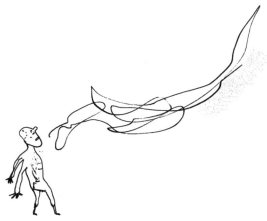

The first time, he asked:
Where were you when I made the Earth? What do you know of the world?

The Earth was wrapped in a sheet of cloud, edged in night and stars; could you have wiped it out?
And the evil ones clinging to the cloth of day, could you eliminate them?

And the indomitable rhinoceros?

And the ostrich, faster than the horse?

The scandal of Creation is not its sufferings, but its freedom.

The second time, God evoked the monsters Behemoth and Leviathan.
Humanity is not the entirety of Creation.
Humble man must also deal with the non-human.

I see that I know you not, said Job. Nor these marvels you have made.

Being innocent, I will accept Creation and its enigma.

And so God raised the face of Job. You have spoken well of me, unlike some others I could name.

And he turned the wheel, returning everything to him in double.

At the end of the night, the world had changed.
Job regained all he had lost, but nothing was the same.

32.

Esther

or The Twist
of Fate

based on *The Book of Esther*

In which a beautiful young woman
saves her people from death by hiding
her origins and marrying a pagan king.
And massacres and feasts follow.

And it came to pass that all were scattered throughout foreign lands.
And God was silent.

The Jews lived hidden in Shushan, the capital of the empire of Persia.

Nothing remained of Jerusalem but the beauty of a small orphan adopted by Mordecai, her cousin.

Beauty that she hid, as she did her Jewish name, Hadassah.

Because she was as beautiful as the night star, they called her Esther.

Her fate was altered when her beauty was discovered by Ahasuerus, the king of the Persians, though it didn't work out so well for Vashti, the sublime queen.

Queen Vashti was supposed to appear for the great imperial feasts.
But for all one hundred and eighty days of the festival, Vashti proudly refused to be seen.

Furious, the king sent her packing. She might influence the other women.

Throughout the empire began the search for a new queen.

Many young women were brought to the royal harem.
At the end of a year, each was brought before the king.

When it was Esther's turn, the king loved her more than any other woman.

Esther became queen. But she said nothing of her roots
and remained secretly faithful to her adoptive father and his people.

And at the entrance to the palace, Mordecai kept vigil.
One day he overheard two guards planning to assassinate the king.

Mordecai denounced them to Esther, who tipped the king off.

The two guards were hanged.

Ahasuerus selected Haman as his vizier, the highest post in the land.

Haman was a descendent of the terrible king of the Amalekites,
the people who had promised to exterminate the Hebrews.

When all were invited to render him homage, Mordecai refused to kneel down.

A Jew kneels before no one but God.

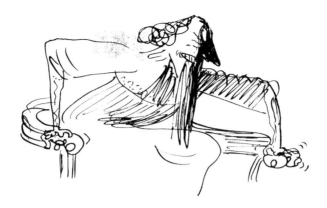

Haman vowed to take these strange foreigners and break their spirit.

He ordered that they all be exterminated.
And their property appropriated.

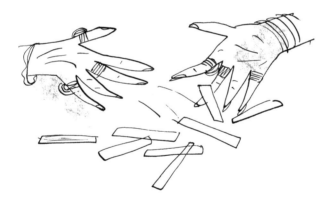

They cast *Pur*, which is to say, lots, to determine the best month to act.
It was *Adar*, the twelfth month, the last.

Panic throughout the kingdom. All the Jews cried. Many fled; others hid.

Mordccai asked Esther to have a word with the king.

Who had not forgotten that Mordecai had saved his life, and was looking for a way to reward him.

Esther invited Haman to a great banquet with the king. And there revealed her roots: She and Mordecai were Jews. Haman wanted them killed.

But because of his love for Esther, the king reversed his order.

And Haman was hanged with his face covered.

A great light washed over the Jewish people. Their lot had taken a turn for the better.

Esther asked the king to allow the Jews to defend themselves from all who were against them.

At Shushan, five hundred men were killed. Among them, Haman's ten sons.

And the next day another three thousand.

In all, seven thousand five hundred throughout the kingdom.

And then peace. To celebrate the end of fear, secrecy, and death, a great carnival was held.

Everyone gave a dinner for their neighbors and the poor.
From that day on, they made the delicious cookies known as hamantaschen—
Hebrew for "Haman's ears."

And ever since, Purim has been celebrated in memory of the fact
that God is present in all matters of chance.

33.

Tobit

or Hope is a Novel

based on *The Book of Tobit*

In which a young man, an angel, and a small dog determine the destiny of old Tobit and of many others in exile. And we learn that the only real debt that we have to collect is that of hope.

An old man, before dying, told this story of misery being overcome by adventure.

A black sun rose over Jerusalem. I, Tobit, was exiled to Nineveh in Mesopotamia.

I left, erasing all our traces. My wife, Anna, and our young son, Tobias, came along.

But I lived with the dead.

The king Sennacherib killed all the sons of Israel,
and every night I searched for the bodies of my brothers to bury them.

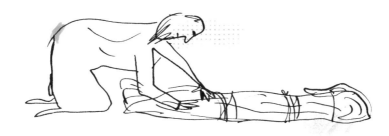

I was so pious in my sorrow that I thought of nothing but the sad demands of my funereal duties.

Every night, digging graves.
While my neighbors watched, laughing.

One evening, I looked up to the skies and got the droppings of a sparrow in my eyes.

Incurable scarring. Like the dead who so obsessed me, I went completely blind.

I asked: Is there no more joy? I'd rather be dead than in such pain.

At the same time in Ecbatana in Media, Sarah, the daughter of Raguel,
having been insulted and mocked, was lamenting.

Seven times married and seven times widowed—and always on the night of her wedding!
The victim of a demon.

Who could cure her anguish?

A young man, a little dog, and an angel.

I remembered some money I'd left with a relative in Ecbatana. Tobias offered to go there to get it.

A stranger, Azariah, appeared and walked along beside him.
We didn't know it, but he was Raphael, the healing angel.

So off they went, angel, dog, and man.

First step: the banks of the Tigris.

Tobias went to wash his feet. And a huge fish leapt out of the water and grabbed him.

Azariah called out: Fear not! Just catch him.

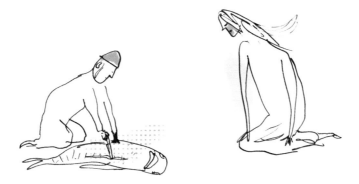

And take out his bile, his heart, and his liver. You'll need them later.

They grilled the rest and had a lovely dinner.

Second step: Ecbatana. The house of Raguel and his daughter Sarah.

Introductions were made. Sarah's sad tale was told.
Who would love her if seven times, death had been the winner?

How about me? Tobias suggested. Raguel accepted, though not without misgivings.

The wedding was held as the dog frolicked in the yard
and the angel retired to a corner, majestic and peaceful.

See Tobias and Sarah heading off to bed.

Azariah asked to have the heart and liver burnt to thwart the demon's curse.

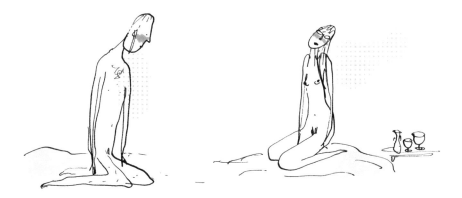

The lovers' prayers:
Tobias: I will do her no harm; I will only love her.
Sarah: You have given me to him like Eve unto Adam, so he'll have a companion.

But Raguel dug a grave for Tobias, just in case.

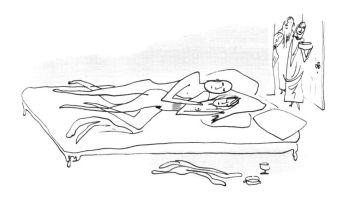

A servant entered the room at dawn. And found the lovers asleep, alive and calm.

Tobias had survived!

Third step: Recover the money. And head back home.

Anna saw them coming and threw herself into the arms of her son.

Tobias took the bile of the fish and rubbed it into my eyes.

I, Tobit, regained my happiness with my sight.

I wanted to reward Azariah, who revealed that he was Raphael, an angel sent by God.

Kings keep their secrets, but God reveals his: To do good is to cure the bad.

Joyous prayer: Jerusalem will be rebuilt. Peace will return.

I, Tobit, tell you that hope is a story.
And that a marvelous tale can heal the world.

34.

Return from Exile

or, Jerusalem, the New City

based on *The Book of Ezra* and *The Book of Nehemiah*

In which, after returning from exile,
they not only reconstruct Jerusalem
but also remember the stories that
gave them hope and helped them live.

For ages, our people had been banished to sad houses not our own.

Exiles, we'd trembled on the shores of the waters of Babylon.

Finally, King Cyrus freed us, and we returned from distant lands.
But in Judah the whole community had to be rebuilt.

How to live together: those who'd returned, those who'd stayed,
and all the others who lived there too?

Those who came back from Babylon with Zerubbabel arrived first.
First job: Reconstruct the altar for sacrifices and feasts.

Then rebuild the Temple.

They gathered tradesman skilled in every sort of work.
And imported wood, stone, and ornaments from all over the world.

Even the young priests joined in.

They gathered more than two hundred singers, four hundred camels,
and six hundred donkeys and organized a feast.

Next came Nehemiah, exiled twenty years in Shushan, the capital of Persia.

One evening, travelers arrived from Jerusalem. Nehemiah asked them:
What news have you of those who stayed? And what of our holy, beloved, and forsaken city?

Its walls have been breached and all the gates burnt.

Nehemiah sat down in the dust and cried.

He cried out to God: Please remember what you promised Moses: *Though there were of you cast out unto the uttermost part of the heaven, yet will I gather them from thence*, and I will bring you home.

Nehemiah said to the king: The city of our fathers' graves is razed.
Let me leave for Jerusalem to rebuild it.

The king said OK. And he gave him trees to use as beams and sent him on his way.

At Jerusalem, the great work had already begun.
They would raise anew the city walls and rebuild all its gates.

Each family and each trade set about the work, patching and repairing.

Some rebuilt the Sheep Gate.

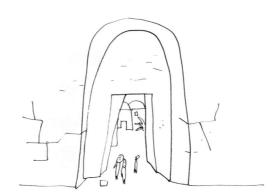

Others, the Fish Gate.

Still others, the Old Gate.

The Furnace Tower.

The Valley Gate.

The Rubbish Gate.

The Gate of the Well.

The huge wall began to rise.
But some people in the city felt threatened and opposed it.

So half the men continued the work, their swords near at hand,
while the other half stood by with pikes and lances.

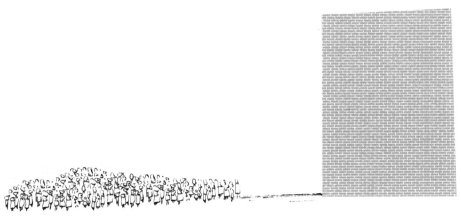

Finally, the wall was done. And all the people gathered around.

They remembered another protective wall, an invisible one:
the stories that, in bad times, had comforted them. The story of our fathers and of Moses.

The scribe Ezra brought out the book.
He mounted a pulpit, and before the standing crowd,

he read the law of Moses aloud.
They paid attention. And felt protected.

Whenever someone reads this book, God is present here with us.

In this book are stories that bring people together. They tell the tale of a people in all their mystery,
and of their role at the heart of the world's history. And of the path of hope.
It's a history of a commitment of unusual depth. But is it really the end of all worry?

35.

Daniel

or There's No End Without a Tomorrow

based on *The Book of Daniel*

In which the end of time is announced along with the end of idols and errors, a time given over to pardon. And we learn that maybe we won't end up exactly as dust after all.

In the silence of the present, the tales of the past and its terrible events must nonetheless be told.
History never ends. All was still dark long after the exile was done.

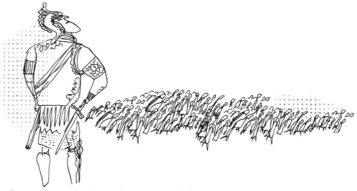

There was Nebuchadnezzar, Babylon's king. And then later, Alexander, king of Macedonia,
Darius, king of Persia, and Antiochus, king of Syria.
They wanted to make everyone live as one under their rule.

There's always a tyrant ready to snatch the stars from the sky and trample them underfoot.

All were forced to bow down to the same ghastly gold statue.
The idol of tyrannical power.

No more hope. Just broken souls.

Collision of time. Rebellion ripe. What fear in us refuses to die?

They had become the smallest nation on Earth. Because they had erred.
To restore hope, they needed to know what had gone wrong.

Within their bruised memories, there arose someone legendary, the young man Daniel.
He was faithful. He read the Scriptures. And understood them.

He had terrifying visions.

The angel Gabriel explained them to him: *O Daniel, I am now come forth to give thee skill and understanding.* It's a time between death and birth.

A quiet space that dreams traverse, in which stories return to haunt us.

Violence never brings an end to violence.

All tyrants want to know the mystery of time and the meanings of dreams.

But magicians and sorcerers never have the answers.

Only God in his heaven can reveal the mystery of the end.

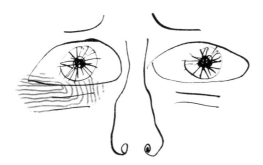

In a vision, Daniel saw four realms of horror, one after the other.

The last was a steel monster that hacked and hewed at everything in its path.

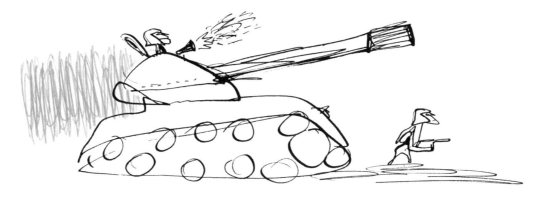

On its head, a horn with a mouth that swore and cursed.

This monster is our history. Of oppression and barbarity. Exile and camps. Walls of hate.

Daniel told the tyrant: Your kingdom, you'll lose it.

Because your kingdom is cruel. But soon, like a cow, you'll be eating grass,

and your hair will turn to the feathers of an eagle,

and your fingers into the raptor's claws.

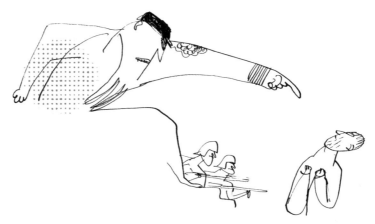

Bow down before me! was the king's only response.

No, before no one but the Lord, the living God.

All who rebel with be thrown to the flames!

But! *What a shock*! Out they walked, openmouthed,
into the heart of the fire, singing and praising God.

An angel exhaled a breeze of dew that pushed the fire back.
Like Daniel thrown into the lion's den,

who came out alive the next day at dawn.
He who believes in the living God subdues all danger with his charm.

So said the angel to Daniel: *Seventy weeks are determined upon thy people and upon thy holy city,
to finish the transgression, and to make an end of sins.*

Enough time to get rid of oppression and evil.
Pardon is the only end possible.

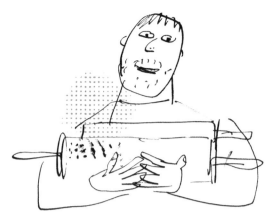

You have the book. Keep it. Read it. The era of the book is the era of the understood.

And he who will come will be neither chief nor prophet nor king;
he will be the Son of man—and he will help everyone understand.

Hope will be reborn. Many who sleep in the land of dust will then wake up.

But isn't it said that man is nothing but dust himself?
Hope and pardon will make something more of him.

Dust that I am.

Writing doesn't end.
Too many stories, books, weak and weary.
In Jerusalem, I was king.
I built palaces and gardens and parks.

But nothing lasts under the sun.
All is vain
and chased by wind.

I've known power and wealth and gold.
But never have I heard the voices of gods.

The gods come disguised
as men but know not
grief nor hope nor
the tremblings of the heart.

Like great girders rotted.
Worms eat their human vestments
but they themselves feel nothing.

Their faces are blackened with smoke
but they themselves feel nothing.
At night in the temples, they're alone
but for the swallows, the bats, and
the errant cats.

They're merchandise.
No breath of life.

They cannot save me from death
nor defend the weak
nor make the blind see
nor aid widow and orphan
nor welcome the foreign
nor render justice
nor love their neighbor.

They are scarecrows in the fields,
thorn bushes in the desert.

Better to live idol-free,
be a man naked in the dust.

And better to believe in the living God
invisible, he who from dust made man,
and from that dust freed man to live.

Readings

CHAPTER 1
The Creation

The "first page" is not the first text written, but the one chosen to open the *Torah*, the five first books of the Hebrew Bible. These texts didn't achieve their definitive form until the Persian era (538–333 BCE). How can the beginning be described when, by definition, no one was there when the world began? The Bible responds to this dilemma in a very original way: The world was made by the word. Ten words of creation named the elements because "the limits of my language are the limits of my world" and of its creation, to borrow a phrase from Ludwig Wittgenstein. To speak is to create our world, to make *the* world into *this* world, the one that is close and known and that I can name. Albert Camus claimed that "to misname an object is to add to the misery of the world." And to name things well increases the happiness of the world. According to the calendar of seven days, the first day was the sole and unique day (*ehad* in Hebrew, as in the expression *Yhwh ehad*, One God), and the seventh day was the day of repose, of interruption. The creation of the world is recounted twice in *The Book of Genesis*. In the first account, humanity, *adam* in Hebrew, exercises power over Creation through kindness (no violence, nor bloodshed, and a vegetarian diet). The *adam* is a collective, both male and female, and intended as a person preceded by an article (*adam* is a play on the word *adamah*—dust, Earth). The *Midrash Rabbah*, written in the fifth century of the Common Era, states: God created the first man as androgynous. And, created in the image of God, man shared in the responsibility of Creation. The beginnings of the world are recounted a second time in chapters 2 and 3 in order to describe the solitude of humanity in the face of Creation. Humanity (*hâ adâm*) doesn't come into its own until the appearance of the woman (*'issâ*), which in turn makes possible the male, the man (*'îs*). Though the animal was truly the first companion that God imagined for the human, it's the woman who appears as the only one capable of coming to the rescue of the human and responding to his solitude. The Hebrew word *'ézèr*, usually translated as "aid," appears in the psalms as meaning the one who comes to our aid—God or his envoy. The rabbi Rachi, in the eleventh century, mischievously adds: "If the *adam* merits it, it will be an aide; if he doesn't, it will be an adversary."

CHAPTER 2
The Garden

This imaginary garden is terrestrial paradise, *'êdén* in Hebrew, a verb that means to live in abundance, in delight. And the Assyrian *edinu* or the Sumerian *edin*: a plain or steppe. This representation is indebted to models developed in ancient centers of erudition such as Memphis, Nineveh, and Babylon (sites to which Jewish scribes and the intellectual and religious elite were exiled after Nebuchadnezzar captured Jerusalem in 597 BCE). This story takes on the tone of a moral tale, a fable about the human condition and human existence. The divinity is first referred to by the word *elohim*, a plural meaning the gods, the divinities. In Semitic languages, *'êl*, "god," is the divine principle of the Syrian-Palestinian pantheons. In these first texts, the double expression *Yhwh elohim*, "Yhwh divinity," also appears, with the four consonants, the tetragram, composing the proper name of the God of Israel. Since the third century BCE, the Jewish people have no longer used the tetragram and have used instead expressions such as *ha-chem*, the Name, or *Adonaï*, Lord. The original pronunciation of the tetragram remains unknown. Modern exegesis has brought it back and pronounces it Yahweh. The Talmud mentions the prohibition placed on pronouncing the word based on the third commandment given to Moses: "*Thou shalt not take the name of the Lord thy God in vain.*" (*The Book of Exodus*, 20:7)

CHAPTER 3
Cain and Abel

Cain and Abel were the first sons of Adam and Eve. The events of the story occur after the expulsion from Eden. The text delivers a very troubling message: The first murder, the first expression of evil, was a fratricide. The older and stronger killed the smaller and "lighter." Abel is often reproached for being *hevel*, in Hebrew, useless, hazy, misty. In other words, he's accused of a certain guilty weakness, a self-effacement, an evanescence. The murder is an expression of jealousy but also of the inability to imagine the position of the other, the inability to recognize him. Many readers have pointed out that Abel never addresses his brother, while Cain would like to speak to Abel. Both Jewish and Christian traditions have tried to understand why God turned away from Cain's gift. "In rejecting his offering," explains Saint Augustine (*City of God*), "God showed him that he should be dissatisfied with himself rather than being unjustly angry with his brother." The resulting violence is an enigma. He who is violent is himself a victim of his impulse and his anger. The violence is compared, in the text, to a beast on the lookout for the man who will be his prey. The Hebrew *rôbês* evokes a crouched beast, ready to leap. After the murder, the "voice of his brother's blood cries from the Earth." The Midrash explains that, as no one had yet been buried, the Earth was scandalized by the spilled blood and absorbed it. But God, by an exceptional sign, protects the guilty and renders vengeance impossible. Cain then suffers both fragility and exile. The great South American writer Jorge Luis Borges has Abel, who has returned from death and run across his brother, say, "Do you know which one of us killed the other? I don't remember." (*In Praise of Darkness*)

Chapter 4
Noah

After Cain, humanity multiplied. And with it, so did violence. "Evil was widespread," says the biblical text. Humanity became "the terror of all creation." This begins a contradictory story dominated by passion, misery, and the Creator's regret. At the beginning of the chapter, the text mentions monstrous and mythological beings that represent the confusion and disorder of the world: The "sons of the gods" sleep with human women, and the *nephilim*, a kind of ogre or giant, roam the land. But how was Noah different? The wise men of the Talmud, the rabbinical

commentaries on Jewish law, have come up with numerous explanations, insisting on Noah's practical wisdom as a builder and farmer. He's even considered humanity's first vintner. And it was he who undertook the strange construction ordered by God. An ark? The Hebrew word *tévah* designates Noah's boat and also, in *The Book of Exodus*, Moses's floating cradle. The word means coffer, box, or even coffin, and the synonym *'arôn* designates the ark of the covenant. The Latin *arca* (*arceo*: that which contains, which encloses) becomes the English word "ark." Since the catacombs, Noah's ark has been represented as a kind of coffer or box. Medieval Christian exegesis emphasizes that there's no mention of a boat for the simple reason that neither navigation nor naval architecture had yet been invented. Historians today interpret it as a three-storied sanctuary like those known to have existed in Mesopotamia. The word "ark" indicates something relatively modest in the face of great catastrophe, a small wooden shelter faced with tremendous unleashed violence. This confirms a beautiful reference to this story in *The Book of Wisdom* 10:4: "*When the Earth was flooded because of him, wisdom again saved it, steering the righteous man by a paltry piece of wood.*" And the humanity that had been "salvaged" was now allowed to kill animals and eat their meat. The ritual of blood finds here its ethical explanation: All blood that is shed is owed to God in memory of this pardon and this new beginning. Humanity must learn to live with its own violence and the knowledge of its own fragility.

Chapter 5
Babel

The various peoples who descended from Noah covered the entire Earth. But some people were opposed to their dispersal. A regressive fantasy of unity and a fear of difference became widespread. The story of a great tower that would shelter all peoples shows up throughout Mesopotamia. This "tower of Babel" suggests a ziggurat, a Babylonian temple with many stories. There's a description of one in Herodotus (c. 485–420 BCE) in his *Histories* (1, 178–186): "And in the middle stood a great tower, measuring one *stade* (125 paces) in length and in width, surmounted by another tower, which in turn, supported a third, and so on, until it reached the eighth. A ramp on the outside spiraled around it all the way up to the final tower." The excessive nature of this structure is associated with the dream of a single language: "*And the whole Earth was of one language (sâphâh), and of one speech*" (*The Book of Genesis*, 11:1). The idea was not just to have a single language, but to speak with a single mouth, a single voice. This text, therefore, effectively denounces the totalitarian follies of our world and the illusion of transparent communication. According to the philosopher Paul Ricoeur, "The myth of Babel is the myth of the destruction of language as the medium of communication." For the Midrash, the construction of the tower demonstrated a devaluation of human life, as, through this collective enterprise, a human life ended up being considered of less value than a brick. Other commentators have suggested that these builders were trying to measure themselves against God. The text plays with a slightly fantastic etymology of the word *babel*, taken from the verb *balal*, which means to scramble, confuse, mix... God prefers hybridity and diversity.

Chapter 6
Abraham

This story follows that of the origin of humanity and its peoples (*The Book of Genesis* 1:11). It focuses on a small group of people, descended from that humanity, that have become scattered all over the Earth. Somewhere south of Mesopotamia, Abraham appeared. One editor decided to open the cycle of the Abraham stories with the tale of the migration from Mesopotamia (Ur) to Canaan (which corresponds, more or less, to what today is Palestine and Israel, with extensions that included parts of Jordan, Syria, Lebanon, and even Egypt). Abraham was a *ger*, a migrant. The word comes up frequently; it indicates a temporary inhabitant, a newcomer who doesn't share in the rights of the residents. It comes from the verb *guwr*, to visit, to be a foreigner, to seek acceptance. It implies someone who has left his land, his family, and

his attachments to respond to a strange call: "*Get thee out of thy country, and from thy kindred, and from thy father's house, unto a land that I will shew thee*" (*The Book of Genesis* 12:1). If the epic of Ulysses is one of nostalgia and the impossibility of returning to the same, Abraham's adventure is one of deracination and the promise of an elsewhere in which he can thrive—and generations of his descendants. Traditionally, Abraham is praised for his obedience and faith. Modernity has questioned this obedience, which could be considered extreme to the point of absurdity. The Danish philosopher Kierkegaard and the writer Kafka share the same insight on patricide. "Abraham's belief was absolutely free of doubt. He believed absurdly," writes Kierkegaard in *Fear and Trembling*, positing that this "knight of the faith" demonstrates the true challenge of "believing because it is absurd." In a parable in his *Journal*, Kafka derails this overly sublime vision, insisting upon the ridiculousness of the character. He evokes Kierkegaard but underscores the "spiritual poverty" of the patriarch whose unforgettable saga is that of the mysterious idiot: "I can conceive of another Abraham who would be ready to respond with the vigor of a café waiter..." In his parodic way, he conjures up a laughable, biblical Don Quixote. This image is reminiscent of the traditional Christian character of the *mad-for-God*, saints and roving madmen at the same time, whose very existence is determined by contradiction. And finally, it must be emphasized that this first promise of land is problematized by the fact that the land is already inhabited by others (*The Book of Genesis* 12:6).

Chapter 7
Abraham and Sarah

This story blends two very well-known incidents: that of Abraham and Sarah's incredulous laughter when they learn that they're going to have a baby and that of Abraham's hospitality, when he welcomes three mysterious strangers into his tent. Double welcome, double hospitality—that of the child to come, though they don't believe it, and that of the foreigners. The promise that ties God to his people hangs upon laughter. This question fascinated all the great Jewish and Christian commentators. As the radical of the verb *tze'hok* expresses more mockery than delight, they have tried to find the reasons behind this laughter—incredulity, surprise, joy, or even revulsion. The two laughters, Abraham's and Sarah's, are the two unexpected passports to the Promised Land. The laughter is rooted in disappointment and derision, expressed by Abraham in the previous chapter: *"And Abram said, Lord God, what wilt thou give me, seeing I go childless"* (*The Book of Genesis* 15:2). The laughter indicates a conflict, a limit "that brings the absolute back into play," according to the biblical scholar Paul Beauchamp. The Hebrew verb, through a play on words, becomes the child's name: Isaac/*yitz'hak* (literally, "He will laugh"). Sarah laughs for what is given "suddenly," for that which has never been possible or accorded. Her laughter acknowledges an impossibility that suddenly makes sense.

Chapter 8
Sodom

This violent story is also one of the most beautiful and the most excessive prayers in the Bible: that of Abraham pleading with God, negotiating with him, to save the city, even if only to spare the lives of the ten innocent people that might be living there. Among the great modern Jewish readers, André Neher and Emmanuel Lévinas consider Abraham in this tale to be "God's worry" in two senses—Abraham is his preoccupation, but Abraham is also resisting him. Abraham pretty much becomes "God's headache." For the philosopher Martin Buber, they are the most stubborn and demanding words ever addressed to God, surpassing even those of Job. Abraham becomes the spokesperson for a lost cause. He defends the exception to extremes. As Pope Benedict XVI said, "... it is not possible to treat the innocent as guilty, this would be unjust; it would be necessary instead to treat the guilty as innocent, putting into practice a 'superior' form of justice." (General Audience of May 18, 2011) Why ten? It's the quorum required for Jewish public prayer. The smaller the number, the greater the mercy of God, the Church Fathers

explain. And the Midrash claims that Abraham should have run after God and continued the negotiations. To which André Neher responds: "Poor Abraham! You don't yet know that God left, not to avoid the end of the dialogue, but to make you run after him and once again harass him toward a decisive bond." (*The Exile of the Word*) And what if Sodom was finally destroyed because Abraham didn't have the strength or the tenacity to plead longer and argue the point even further? And then there's another dramatic scene of hospitality: Lot welcomes into Sodom God's messengers, whom the crowd is pursuing. In the King James Version, the crowd demands the men because they want to "know them"; in the New American Standard version, the phrase used is "have relations with them"; and in the Living Bible, the crowd shouts to Lot: "Bring out those men to us so we can rape them." (*The Book of Genesis* 19:5) The destruction of Sodom is the response to a refusal to welcome the other, the unknown (both the passing foreigner and the enigmatic presence of God). In the Talmud, it's at Sodom that humanity violates the law of hospitality for the first time. The true sin here is the violation of the rights of foreigners.

Chapter 9
Abraham and Isaac

This is the darkest and the most archaic of the Abraham stories. The tradition of human sacrifice and even the sacrifice of children existed in Judah and in the earliest versions of the religion of Yahweh. Abraham appears once again as the most obedient of believers, he "who submits" says the Koran (III, 67), ready to sacrifice his own son if God asks it of him. It is a terrible test of faith, and leads to desolation. Does man grow through submitting himself to the unknown that dominates him, or does this unknown make man greater by leading him to recognize the shadows within himself? Abraham's obedience is exemplary but implausible because the order to sacrifice his own son contradicts the numerous promises of progeny that characterize the alliance between him and God. According to certain interpreters,

God did not explicitly ask Abraham to sacrifice his son. The expression in Hebrew is fairly ambiguous. And some commentators in the Midrash consider, as did Kafka later, that Abraham could have misunderstood the divine order. The text is a true test of our understanding, and its tradition is perhaps rooted in a denunciation of the practice of human sacrifice. Contemporary interpretations address our own desire for crime and our propensity for understanding evil and violence rather than opposing it. What do we understand about God's order? What criminal voices, what destructive words do we obey? Numerous rabbinical commentaries claim that time on the mountain was suspended just as the divine promise was suspended in the murderous urge of the father. Following Saint Augustine (*Sermons on the Old Testament*, II, 5), it can be said that God, in this story, "thus reveals Abraham to himself"—in his doubt as well as in his hope.

Chapter 10
Jacob and Esau

This is another tale of violence at the heart of brotherhood, and revolves around an ancient terror caused by the figure of twins, which often gave rise, as here, to a tale almost carnivalesque or burlesque, a farce, in which the sacred and the tragic become confounded. Jacob, the weak, and Esau, the strong, are the twin sons of Isaac and Rebecca, and the ancestors of two peoples, Édom (which means red, as Esau was red and ate red lentils) and Israel, the name that Jacob took later. At the same time, the tribe of Isaac began to take (too?) great a place in the Promised Land, so Isaac adopted the migratory life that his father, Abraham, had led. Each well that he passes is a symbolic encounter and a reminder of the promise of God. In the scene of the stolen blessing, the tragic story takes off into farce: Isaac mistakes the pelt of a goat for his son, who was known to be exceptionally hairy. Once the deception is discovered, Jacob is forced to flee his brother's hatred.

Chapter 11
Jacob's Battle

"A strange adventure, mysterious from beginning to end . . . Philosophers and poets, rabbis and storytellers, have all tried to resolve the enigma of what happened that night." (Elie Wiesel, *Celebrations, Portraits, Legends*) It begins with Jacob's dream of a strange ladder, no doubt inspired by the great stairways of the Mesopotamian ziggurats that symbolize an ascension to heaven. The stone that he raises in remembrance of this dream is, according to the Talmud, the first stone of the first house ever built on Earth. Later in his flight from his brother's vengeance, Jacob has to cross a great river. In ancient and popular literature, the crossing of a ford is always an initiatory moment. As a test, Jacob spends the entire night in confrontation with a stranger (an angel? God himself?). From this struggle, he gains a blessing and a new name. He becomes Israel, which means "God prevails" or "he who fights with God." Israel was the name of the kingdom until the death of Solomon. According to the Midrash, Jacob, weak and fearful, thus becomes the bearer of a great blessing and an extraordinary vision. The tale of the combat is told in eight enigmatic verses. Is Jacob fearful or courageous? Is he fighting with the unknown or against it? And who actually won? "A happy battle in which God is vanquished by man," said Victor Hugo. For Rachi, in the eleventh century, the most important element was Jacob's fear. He tries to soften his brother up with gifts but must confront his own fear, which is revealed by the angel, as if the confrontation that didn't occur between the two brothers must take place in a dream. The *Midrash Rabbah* emphasizes that Jacob and his adversary "fall into each other" as one falls asleep. The Jewish philosopher Maimonides (1138–1204) also thought that Jacob's fight might have taken place in a dream. The unknown entity is initially referred to in Hebrew as *ish*, a man, but at the end of the struggle, Jacob speaks of a god (*elohim*). The fight, the confrontation, had to be embodied in order for it to become a recognition and a deliverance. Elie Wiesel sees, in this figure, Jacob's guardian angel, who fights with "the I within him, who doubted his mission."

Chapter 12
Joseph in Egypt

The object of biblical stories is often to show how certain men falsely accuse others, their brothers, of some evil and then use this as a pretense to hate them, persecute them, and even kill them. This is the case with the story of Joseph and his brothers, which closes *The Book of Genesis*. But it's different from the other tales of patriarchs, in that God intervenes very little. Joseph's destiny is worthy of a novel—sold by his own brothers into slavery, he is imprisoned in Egypt, only to be raised to the rank of the viceroy of a great, idolatrous, and polytheistic empire. Jacob had twelve sons. Joseph was his favorite, which incited the jealousy of his brothers, who nicknamed him, in derision, "the dreamer." He was a talented interpreter of dreams, which was a sign of power, and this talent occasioned his downfall before it, in the long run, saved him. The conflict between Joseph and his brothers, who are under the authority of Judah, one of the twelve tribes of Israel, became the root of two royal dynasties of Hebrew peoples, the kingdom of Israel and the kingdom of Judah. For the Torah, this tension is much more than a simple family feud. It illustrates the confrontation of two different Jewish destinies. Joseph's is marked by sharing with the outside world. According to the Talmud, Joseph was *Yossef ha-tsadik*, Joseph the Just. And, stained with blood, thrown down a well, and then sold, he became, for the Church Fathers, a prefiguration of the Passion of Christ. This unlikely tale of a Judean exile's successful assimilation into a foreign culture, a slave who became a king, was probably created by a Jewish diaspora Hellenized in Egypt and opposed to the institution of the Temple of Jerusalem. Joseph never claimed he would return to the Promised Land. He took an Egyptian name and an Egyptian wife (the daughter of a great priest), worked for the Pharaoh, and collected taxes. Egypt, one of the most Judeo-phobic countries of antiquity, is, in

this case, a land of welcome and prosperity before becoming, in *The Book of Exodus*, a terrible "house of slavery." According to the Midrash, Joseph occupied a unique place in universal history; he knew seventy languages and was literally immersed in other peoples: *nivla bein ha-oumot* ("swallowed among the peoples").

Chapter 13
Joseph and his Brothers

This story bears witness to how much the Bible owes to Egypt; in it, Jacob/Israel, the great patriarch, ends by moving himself and his whole family there. Joseph acquired an astonishing symbolic position as the "feeder" of the people. For Rachi, he became the Pharaoh's double. Some rabbis consider that Joseph must have been masked, like an Egyptian god; otherwise, his brothers would have recognized him. The text insists on the distress of the elderly Jacob, who remained in Canaan, starving and deprived of his sons. The end of the story is determined by Joseph himself and by his capacity to forgive. "*But as for you, ye thought evil against me; but God meant it unto good, to bring to pass, as it is this day, to save much people alive.*" (*The Book of Genesis* 50:20) In the entry on Joseph in his *Philosophical Dictionary*, Voltaire presented him as a "model . . . one of the most precious monuments of antiquity." The story of Joseph "who pardons" is much more moving than that of Ulysses, "who takes vengeance." Between 1926 and 1943, Thomas Mann devoted three wonderful novels to Joseph and his brothers. For Mann, the crucial issue was that a people that could have been founded on fratricide was instead founded on forgiveness. Egypt saved by Joseph is the symbol of a cosmopolitan humanity. In his novel, Mann focuses on the biblical humanism of a society based upon the opposite of murder. "Life without spirit ends in inhumanity," he wrote. Starting with a basis in racial theory and a degree of anti-Semitism, his study of psychoanalysis, religions, and biblical exegesis eventually led him, a reactionary and apolitical writer, into exile and then into support for Franklin D. Roosevelt's social democracy. Thomas Mann, at the height of the

Nazi period, claimed that Judaism and the Jewish civilization founded on the Book constituted one of European civilization's sources of rational thought and ethics, and was one of the sources of humanism for a global civilization.

CHAPTER 14
Moses

Joseph's generation passed, and the situation became dramatically reversed. Egypt and Israel had ceased to be close. The Egyptians were afraid of the people of Israel, who prospered among them. While in *Genesis* the promise was life, suddenly the Pharaoh wanted to thwart life. The story of Moses is the tragic illustration of this paradox. The son of two cultures (his name has Egyptian roots), a newborn Hebrew condemned to death by Egypt, he owed his life to an Egyptian princess, but had to fight to the death against Egypt in order to liberate his people from slavery. The story of his birth echoes the legend of King Sargon, no doubt in order to give him a status as prestigious as that of the sovereign who unified Mesopotamia. It was to Moses, forced to flee through the desert and the mountains after having killed an Egyptian soldier, that God revealed his name in a burning bush. The Church Fathers point out that God showed himself through the most hostile and meager thing in the desert, thus evoking commentaries in the Midrash: "Why did God choose to speak to Moses from a bush? To prove that nowhere in the world is devoid of divine Presence, not even a bush." The bush symbolizes the destitution of Israel in Egypt, and God wanted to show himself in deprivation and humility. "Just as a bush is lesser than a tree, so the sons of Israel have been diminished in Egypt, which is why God saved them." God gave his name in a form that has become famous: 'ehyeh 'ashér 'ehyeh, literally "I am: I will be" or "I am that I am." Yahweh is, by definition, Existence or Being.

CHAPTER 15
The Liberation of the People

The Exodus as it is recounted in the Bible left no traces in Egyptian documents, though the name of Israel is found on a stele of Ramses II's successor, Merneptah, that dates from around 1220 BCE. "This story is so amazing that it is known all over the world," said Origen as early as the third century. The image of slavery in Egypt has struck the imagination of many oppressed peoples. This epic tale of liberation is the foundation of the history of Israel, the one that everyone must remember. But first, it's a dark and terrifying story in which God, in order to liberate his people, gets involved in a terrible and mortal bidding war. The end of the story is key: Once free, the Hebrews must look back on the dead bodies of the Egyptians strewn across the shore of the Red Sea. This traumatizing image was so gripping that in the *Book of Isaiah* God reminds the people: "*I gave Egypt for thy ransom.*" (*The Book of Isaiah* 43:3) The description of the forced labor, with the Hebrew overseers who had to survey and punish their brothers, has a painful resonance with the camps of the twentieth century. The slaves even reproached Moses for having engendered the hatred of the Pharaoh to the point that they acquired a bad smell. "You have made our smell bad." The smell of liberty was execrable to the tyrant, claims Origen in his commentary on *Exodus*. God sent Egypt nine initial plagues, or more precisely, strikes (*nega* in Hebrew, comes from the verb *naga*, to strike or to hit). Some of the plagues made a humiliating allusion to the strength of Egypt: the divine Nile turning into a river of blood and the devastating plague of frogs, which makes a reference to the goddess Heqet. The tenth strike killed all the firstborn children, finally allowing the people of Israel to escape. It was the night of Passover. The Hebrew word means "passage" or "leap." Death passed over and did not strike the houses of the Hebrews. It was a night of death and a night of deliverance that would not be forgotten. It was the Hebrew *Zakkhor*, the "Remember-this," on which Judaism is founded. Remember what God had to do to save Israel— which is to say, the unthinkable, the unimaginable.

CHAPTER 16
The Ten Commandments

This story tells of freedom tested by desire. It begins with a long march through the desert up to the mountain where God showed himself to Moses and gave him the tablets of the Law. Along the march, freedom had created fear and made the people impatient. They demanded something to eat and drink. In response to their aggravated desire, a strange bread fell from the sky—so strange that the people cried out, "What's that?" (*man hu*, in Hebrew, from which the word "manna" comes). However, to God, this fearful, recalcitrant people was a treasure, from a Hebrew word, *segullâh*, which means jewel, joyous, and domain, all at once. There are two versions of the Ten Commandments in the Torah, one in *The Book of Exodus* and the other in *Deuteronomy*. Seven of the Ten Commandments are negative. This was the way that the people, after their liberation, learned about their responsibilities—toward God and toward others. The people built their identity on fundamental human values before they had attained material or political solidity and long before they had established a royalty or conquered the land. "On this point, the Bible shows itself to be extraordinarily modern," says the exegetist Jean-Louis Ska.

CHAPTER 17
The Golden Calf

The cult of the calf or of the bull was widespread in the ancient east; the animal symbolized fertility and fecundity and was celebrated with orgiastic rites. This was echoed in Egypt, with the goddess Hathor, and in Greece, with the Minotaur. The people preferred a golden idol, a visible representation, to the disquieting silence of God. They wanted something that they could see, and right away, rather than the gift of the tablets on which God had written the Ten Commandments. Writing figures in this tale in a way that is almost unprecedented in antiquity—it constitutes the force of and the point of contact with the divinity. Moses died on the threshold of the Promised Land. He saw it from afar, but never got there. *Scripsit et abiit*, as Saint Augustine said in his confessions (XI, 3, 5): "He has written [the Torah, because Antiquity had made Moses its author], and is now gone." Nothing remained but the writing. The gift of the Law is also the gift of writing as trace and as memory. Texts in the Bible and the Midrash ask of what fault Moses could possibly have been guilty that he was not allowed to reach the Promised Land. From a contemporary perspective, it seems that, in the return from exile in Babylon, Israel needed to create a figure that had founded institutions (a culture, a code of law, and alliances), and a system of ethics in order to justify its existence in light of its lack of a monarchy or political autonomy.

CHAPTER 18
Jericho

Though they attained the Promised Land, they did so only by unprecedented cruelty. The existing, native populations were almost entirely exterminated. Moses's successor, Joshua, became a pitiless warrior and general. The macabre litanies that describe it all have raised serious questions for rabbis who don't agree with the demand for exclusion and extermination, and yet also don't acknowledge the perspectives of the other Canaanite populations. The Jewish philosopher Maimonides (1138–1204) emphasizes that each city was offered the possibility to surrender and thereby save its people: "The Torah demands that each city be called to peace, as seeking peace is a virtue in itself." And the Talmud of Jerusalem says, "Joshua issued an ultimatum to each area that he wanted to conquer, stating that those who wanted to leave could leave and those who wanted to make peace were invited to do so." To contemporary historians, these stories seem in line with the literary conventions and nationalistic propaganda of the era and are modeled after the warrior tales of the Assyrians and the Neo-Babylonians. They needed to turn Yahweh into a warlord facing the threat of great military empires. This intention is confirmed by an initial version of these stories written toward the end of the Judean monarchy in the seventh century BCE. And the vivid facts recounted, such as the fall of the walls of Jericho, are closer in tone to a fable than to a responsible historical chronicle. Modern archeology has shown that at the time of the conquest of Canaan (1400–1200 BCE), Jericho did not have fortified walls, and so this conquest was probably not made in the manner of a *blitzkrieg*. There is no archeological trace of such an invasion. The tale of the battle relies heavily on details either imagined or invented: the River Jordan stops, suspended; a mysterious warrior angel fights alongside the Hebrews; Jericho falls to the blasts of ritual trumpets without a single blow being struck, and the sun and moon stop and hang motionless in the sky for the entire duration of the battle. And what's more, the capture of Jericho was only possible thanks to Rahab, who was not only an enemy Canaanite, but also a woman and a prostitute. Joshua later married Rahab, whose name is found in the genealogy of Christ that opens *The Book of Matthew*.

Chapter 19
Ruth

The book of Ruth is a fairy tale, and is, in Paul Claudel's words, that of *"Ruth la rusée,"* which might be translated as "Ruth the Ruthlessly Resourceful." But its fairy tale quality should not be allowed to eclipse the extraordinary density of this "little story," which took place in the time of the first chiefs of Israel. Here again, a foreigner, an enemy Moabite, is called upon to participate in the destiny of Israel. In fact, she became the ancestor of King David. The affair seems particularly strange in that whoever first wove the tale must have known that the Moabites were barred from converting: *"An Ammonite or Moabite shall not enter into the congregation of the Lord; even to their tenth generation shall they not enter into the congregation of the Lord for ever . . ."* (*The Book of Deuteronomy* 23:3) This is repeated in The Book of Nehemiah 13:1: *"the Ammonite and the Moabite should not come into the congregation of God for ever."* Ruth, the

foreigner, was related to Naomi by marriage—she married Naomi's son. The verb *davaq*—to be linked, attached, to, resistant to—recurs frequently in the text to define Ruth's attitude. Naomi is an emblematic character, forced by famine to leave Bethlehem (the "city of bread" and of King David) with her family. She later returns, ruined, widowed, and without children. It's in the gesture of return, which is a return to herself, and at the very point at which her trials threaten to bury her in her own bitterness, that, thanks to the foreign presence of Ruth, she becomes reconciled to life. The Midrash claims that Ruth and Naomi became so close that they became indistinguishable. Through the character of Boaz, the book addresses generosity and the opening of love. *"Sa gerbe n'était point avare"* ("His wheat, in no way sparse"). (Victor Hugo) The name of Boaz plays on *'oz*, which means strength and power, and on *azah*, goodness.

Chapter 20
Samson and Delilah

This is a well-known story with multiple sources, both Mesopotamian and Greek, in which a hero truly worthy of the ancient epics appears in Israel. His name is related to a number of sun gods and their myths. Samson was deft with fire (war, violence) and the gaze (seduction). Samson "protected the people of Israel like a shield" says the Midrash. The story takes place in troubled times; the royalty had not yet been established and relations among peoples had broken down. "Liberators" appeared, but they often didn't work out very well. Who really was Samson? The Talmud suggests that, as "a clandestine combatant," he was forced to hide his strength by playing the Don Juan. It was said that he destroyed whole armies with a single gesture, and Elie Wiesel claimed that he wiped out the Philistines' fields solely "for personal reasons rooted in his romantic intrigues." His tragic end would be seen today as a kind of "suicide mission." He was killed at Gaza, crying, "I will die among the Philistines!" Some have said that he is but the "caricature of a hero." A *nazir*, an ascetic consecrated to God, he instead ran after girls. He got lost in his prodigious powers and ended up as a destroyer rather than as a savior. Elie Wiesel, in *Prophetic Celebrations*, described the story as "The destiny of the hero who, instead of triumphing over destiny, fails in his mission." And yet . . . let's save the hero Samson! His failure illustrates that of the era, as it waited for its king. Its weakness was human, all too human. He desired all the women who, by their charms, forced him to reveal the secrets of his power. At the end, he was blind, his eyes torn out, a cruel symbol of his desire to see. The text states that when he met Delilah, "He saw her and he loved her." According to the Midrash, the name Delilah comes from *dâlal*, which means impoverished, weakened. Paul Claudel recalls her amorous comment in the *Songs*: "I am black and so beautiful."

Chapter 21
Samuel and Saul

How does one become king? The Hebrew people, who wanted to be like other people, were jealous of the symbol of power constituted by the institution of royalty. The Midrash lists three obligations of the people in the Promised Land: name a king, eliminate the descendants of the enemy Amalek people, and construct a temple. Samuel, "the founder of royalty," as one reads in the Apocrypha (*Sirach* 46: 13–20), is considered in the Talmud as "one of the princes of humanity," comparable to Moses. Samuel tried to dissuade the people from taking on a king, but had to recognize Saul, the unknown young man that God sent to him to be crowned. Their relationship illustrates the ambivalence of this desire for royalty. Saul, from the beginning, hesitates, and hides when he is supposed to be enthroned. Having become king in spite of himself, and a formidable military leader, he defies Samuel's oracle, which demanded the total extermination of the Amalekites, the hereditary enemy of the people of Israel since the Exodus, and decides to spare their king. They were the *reshit goyim*, the first people. The Amalekites could have destroyed the weaker Hebrews from behind, after they had crossed the Red Sea. In contemporary rabbinical literature, the Amalekites

are connected to the memory of the Shoah and to the attempts at extermination that have pursued the Jewish people. But as the philosopher David Banon has said, "Amalek is also an internal dimension of Judaism, when self-doubt becomes dominant." This is the tragic destiny of Saul, who has a rendezvous with the fratricidal hatred of origins, with a desire for extermination, both his own and the other's. God sends him an "evil spirit." The story of his fall is a key event in Israel's invention of the political. But Saul chose to listen to his heart, the Midrash believes. He would have even refused to kill civilians and animals . . . His error? He wanted to be more just than necessary or possible—this was his ruin, his folly. The folly of King Saul is the price of these transformations. The true tragedy was that the king, the madman, the musician, and the giant (Goliath) all met in a confrontation of Shakespearean proportions.

Chapter 22
David and Goliath

The ambivalent relationship between the prophet Samuel and Saul was followed by a no less ambiguous and tragic one between Saul and David. At first, Saul welcomed the young shepherd and musician because he could sooth his melancholy with his playing and singing. Then the young shepherd became a national hero by defeating the giant Goliath, after which, David was made king. And the tragedy unfolds: Saul becomes jealous and criminally dark-minded. Royalty in Israel was born in blood, familial war, and melancholy. But the figure of David is founded on the celebrated biblical myth that gives victory to the weak over the strong, to the young over the monstrous, to a shepherd armed with a slingshot over a heavily armed soldier. King David needed a legend to support and explain him. In another biblical text (*The Second Book of Samuel* 21:9), the victory over Goliath is attributed to a different hero, Elhanan of Bethlehem. Numerous commentaries in the Midrash claim that David and Goliath were enemy cousins, with David being the descendent of Ruth the Moabite and Goliath the descendent of her sister Orpah.

Chapter 23
David and Bathsheba

Saul, the defeated king, passed the position on to David. David became the great king of Israel, and his legend became extremely important in Judaic history and for political theology in medieval Christianity. However, his path was not straight: crime, lies, manipulation, treachery... This story shows that David was at the heart of a true court society with all its spies and intrigues; it also shows the way in which the beginning of a monarchic dynasty was eclipsed by an error and a crime committed with the woman who became the dynastic mother of the great king Solomon: Bathsheba. The story of the adultery between David and Bathsheba, the wife of Uriah, the faithful Hittite soldier, whom David wanted dead, poses serious problems for interpreters. The rabbinical tradition has worked indefatigably to justify David, or even to pardon him and clean up his image, going as far as to claim that Bathsheba was destined for David since the beginning of the world.

Chapter 24
Elijah at Horeb

The appearance of this unforeseen prophet is an event in the great biblical story of salvation and the promise. He came out of nowhere. No one was waiting for him, nor had his coming been announced. He was a man alone from the beginning to the end. He opposed King Ahab and Queen Jezebel (ninth century BCE), who are described with truly biblical exaggeration as impious and idolatrous rulers, devoted to the cult of Baal, a Canaanite deity. This was a heresy and an abomination for the Israeli writers who had come back from exile, and Elijah did his best to eliminate it. Elijah was headstrong, impossible. Isolated by his flight from the anger of Queen Jezebel, he accused her people of having abandoned their alliance with God. According to the rabbis, God replied: "You're right to remember that it's not your alliance, but mine! What business is it of yours?" Elijah also witnessed a great prophetic transformation. God made a dramatic appearance,

intervening for the last time in a fiery faceoff with Baal, while to Elijah, he revealed himself as the softness of silence. God attends to his people in ways other than through a show of force. Elijah retraces Moses's path through the desert to freedom, a lonely path until God reveals himself to him silently. "If you truly want to free someone, be silent." (Maurice Maeterlinck, *The Treasure of the Humble*) In Hebrew, the phrase *qol demamah daqaq* indicates a voice, a noise, a call (*qol*) in an agonizingly soft murmur, in silence (*demanah*), like dust, powder, finely ground (*daqaq*): a voice of fine silence. The agonizing noise ends in a silence like dust. Martin Buber translated it as "an evaporating voice." Silence is no longer a sign of God's anger or refusal. "In his solitude, the prophet Elijah learns that it's the god of silence and retreat that is the living god." (André Neher) It's also in this sense that the protestant theologian Dietrich Bonhoeffer suggested that to be silent is to preach the presence of God. (*Course in Christology*, 1933) According to the Talmud, Elijah announced the coming of the Messiah; the evangelists make several references to it. And according to a Midrashic tradition, God told Elijah that no circumcisions would occur among the people of Israel unless he was present. For Passover and the ceremony of circumcision, the Jewish people always include an empty chair and leave a door ajar to symbolize their expectation of his return.

Chapter 25
Solomon and the Queen of Sheba

Solomon (c. 970–933 BCE) succeeded David. His material and political success and, above all, his construction of the Temple made him the ideal model of a king. But this monarch, mad for wisdom, also turned toward idolatry, which resulted in the division and destruction of his kingdom. The Temple, built by Solomon, was destroyed by Nebuchadnezzar in 586 BCE, and part of the Judean elite was exiled to Babylon. Why such a setback? No doubt because the divine promise goes beyond mere material and political success. And because this model of a king is explained in relation to wisdom, which began everything. "*Wisdom was created before all other things*," states *Sirach* (1:4). With King Solomon, wisdom is linked to royalty. But can one possess wisdom as one possesses glory or material goods? And how is wisdom desired? What is more seductive than wisdom? The first trial was the Temple, the house of God and of Wisdom. "The Temple is the embellishment of the world, in that it represents the very essence of beauty on Earth. And thus it makes the spiritual relationship between God and man possible," wrote the philosopher Henry Corbin. But the presence of God in his house among men depends largely on the hearts of men. Solomon seduced the beautiful foreign queen of Sheba, who had come from the farther reaches of the world. Solomon, seducer and idolater, also seduced foreign women into his harem in Jerusalem. The encounter with the queen of Sheba has generated an impressive amount of popular literature. In the Apocrypha, it is said that the queen arrived with strange animals that no one had ever seen before, and that Solomon, in his great wisdom, bowed down before them. Another tradition suggests that the "animals" to which Solomon bowed were in fact foreign and "strange" pagans. The legend, thus, focuses on foreignness and points to the fact that foreigners recognized the great wisdom of Israel, proof of its sovereignty over all creation, known and unknown, real and imaginary. Again according to the Apocrypha, the queen of Sheba was more than enthralled, which justifies the next event in the series, in which Solomon admits his tremendous weakness for beautiful foreigners, with which he has filled his harem. He was confronted by the enigma of his own desire, which was at once both wise and mad.

CHAPTER 26
Love Scenes

For the Pharisees of the first century, during the time of Jesus, the scroll of the *Song of Songs* did not have a place in the liturgy of the synagogue. It was the rabbi Aqiba who declared this enigmatic poem the "holy of holies" of Scripture, and wrote:

"The world had no value and no meaning before the poem of poems was given to Israel." Christians had to wait for the allegorical readings of the Fathers before the text was accepted into their community prayer. In Hebrew *sîr ha sîrîm* literally means the "song of songs" or the "best of songs." *Sîr* is a poem, a song of joy and love. There are even those who think that it was composed by women. The Jewish tradition claimed that the key to the text had been lost, and emphasized the absence of any explicit theological reference. It is first of all a love song in the manner of the erotic poetry of the Near East, both Sumerian and Egyptian. It has been attributed to Solomon, which is clearly not accurate, but that attribution has become an integral part of the poem itself, and supports the image of a king who could be dedicated to wisdom and the spirit as well as to pleasure and delight, a king who built temples and yet became the central figure of a song and could understand the mysteries of love. This poem is undoubtedly a compilation of the love songs of the time, with different refrains and amorous motifs, which was a method frequently used in antique and medieval literature. But it's also a dramatic and theatrical composition, which many, from Ernest Renan to Paul Beauchamp to Paul Claudel, have emphasized. It features unidentified characters addressing each other directly: The Lover or the Shulamite (the *Midrash Rabbah* gives four derivations of this name, all of them related to *shalom*, peace), King Solomon, the shepherd lover, the daughters of Jerusalem, and the soldiers. It's a fragmented story, a dream story with a midnight chase through the city, a story in which a woman imprisoned in a harem escapes to search for her lover. In this wonderful poem, love has a rendezvous with Wisdom; it signifies the love of love, a theme found in all great mystical literature, such as *Dark Night of the Soul* by Saint John of the Cross. The mystery, the *eros*, of this text has been retained, especially in the celebrated line "Love is as strong as death"— literally *ki'aza khamavet ahava*, love is as inexorable as death. "This death, which is to say love," adds Meister Eckhart. Vertigo.

Chapter 27
Isaiah's Visions

What is a *nabi*, or prophet (according to the Greek translation)? One who sees, not the future, but the Word of the story in the process of creating itself and becoming embodied. He sees what no one wants to see and yet is right before everyone's eyes. A prophet quite different from the traditional prophets of the ancient east, he did not practice divination or magic, but described the tragic present of the people in the word of God. The biblical prophet, explains Paul Beauchamp, maintains the rapport between the received word and the act, between the Word and history. This is the central theme of the book of Isaiah: The people have lost the voice of God, lost contact with the founding narrative, and above all with the values of justice associated with the liberation of the people and the foundation of royalty. The book of Isaiah is a compilation of prophetic statements and predictions gathered over more than half a century and collected into a unified text about the return from exile. Isaiah was active in Jerusalem between 740 and 701 BCE. He was an influential person who knew royal politics well, a seer and a counselor, who was not punished despite his extremely violent remarks about King Hezekiah's politics, which consisted in playing Egypt off against Ashur, and then submitting to Ashur. In the Talmud, it is claimed that Hezekiah might have become the king chosen by God as messiah and that the war waged by the Assyrian kings could have been the final war. But Isaiah shifted the emphasis of his predictions onto the social situation, justice, and the law, formulating a virulent critique of hypocritical cult-based powers and practices. This diverse book covers the most violent trials: the division of the kingdom of David, the crisis of royalty, wars (with Assyria and Egypt), and the deportation of huge numbers of people, first to the north (722 BCE and the annexation of the Assyrian empire), then to the south (the attempt by Sennacherib in 701 to capture Jerusalem). Isaiah seems, in fact, to be several people. One Isaiah rises up against Judah and Jerusalem after the defeat of the northern kingdom in the context of the war with Assyria.

Another is a bearer of hope when all is dark, reminding a crowd of people of Yahweh's promise for a reign of universal peace, and yet another tries to convince the deportees of the imminence of salvation and suggests the enigmatic figure of a messiah outside traditional royalty, a suspicious and suspected figure whose mysterious sign is his anonymity and unrecognizability. He is an *ebed*, a servant, a slave, and yet the word also means "messiah," awaited king. The words of the prophet are addressed not only to the powerful but also to the *'anawim*, literally, the downtrodden, the cowed, the crushed, the victims and the forgotten of history, both past and that to come.

Chapter 28
Ezekiel's Visions

A small man, suitcase in hand, incarnates the universal silhouette of the exile, the deported. He left while those who stayed in Jerusalem watched. Considered the last prophet, he marks the rupture with the ancient world. He foretold a universal God whose word would touch all of human history, even to the detriment of the prophet who remained silent. The prophet of resilience and imagination, Ezekiel was a priest (or the son of a priest) of Jerusalem whose ministry was carried out in Babylon during the exile. According to the book's prologue, this occurred in the fifth year of exile (593 BCE). The book describes a symbolic itinerary through both time and space, in both imagination and reality, reminiscent of Dante's *Divine Comedy*. Ezekiel is a kind of shaman who goes beyond the usual shamanistic characteristics. He recounts several divine oracles, which he received in the form of elaborate visions, embellished with trances and geographical and physical transports. The central great vision of the book (chapter 37), that of the valley of dried bones and their return to life, symbolizes the announcement of the return from exile, the restoration of the nation of David, and the reconstruction of the Temple, and is, in addition, a universal eschatological vision. Ezekiel insisted upon the division between the small community of the deported (the priests and the administrative elite) and the major part of the population of Judah that remained in the country. The character of Ezekiel is enigmatic: Was he really a priest or was he a usurper? He claimed that he was called to prophesy, but did so in an excessively charismatic way, making maximum use of his strange gifts. Ezekiel's visions ended up at the heart of great esoteric traditions, and as such they've often been considered by the Talmudic tradition to be dangerous to interpret. It is said that the vision of the celestial chariot at the beginning of the book, in particular, represents one of the most difficult secrets of the Bible. And the Talmud doubts the truth of the vision of the dried bones, underscoring the ambiguity of any oracle and the importance of not seeing just a simple parable or inventive tale: *mashal haya*.

Chapter 29
Jonah

This is the history of a minor, depressive prophet, the story of a fall from grace, *yarad* in Hebrew, incorporating a series of detours: toward the city of Jaffa, in the hold of a ship, in sleep, in the belly of a fish, and in the abyss of despair. It most probably dates from the time of the exile. This prophet had only one mission: to go to talk to the non-Jews in Nineveh, the capital of Assyria, the enemy of Israel. What was Jonah fleeing? In Jewish communities, his story is told on Yom Kippur, at the end of the day, when the faithful pray to the Eternal, asking him to finally pardon him. What pardon does this refer to? Is it the one from his people that Jonah could not bring himself to give to his enemies, or is it Jonah's own pardon, the one that he did not want to receive? "Jonah is a frustrated prophet," claims Elie Wiesel. If he didn't immediately obey God, it was because he dreaded the possible pardon accorded to a criminal. What's at stake in this story is repentance and reversal (*teshouvah*). The lot of the malicious is never settled, which is a tragedy for the Just. In the Midrash, Jonah is also described as truly just, one of the rare people to enter paradise while still alive. According to the ancient Jewish tradition, it was for love of his people that Jonah decided not

to go to Nineveh; he feared that the conversion of the people of Nineveh could be twisted into a motive for the condemnation of Israel. And so he had to confront his own grievances, his own frustrations. He was swallowed by "a great fish," inside of which he gave himself over to prayer and to a kind of introspection. The prophet traversed the night of faith, which is confirmed by the psalm of supplication that he recited in the abyss. What love means is the real question here. Jonah's theological problem is that of his "depression." Jonah is incapable of accepting the effects of pardon; he can't manage to get out of himself. The reaction of the king and the people of Nineveh is unprecedented in the entire Hebrew Bible, and Jonah's reaction is also completely surprising. Embedded in this moving and rather amusing story is the grandeur of compassion: to care for the life of the other, of the guilty, of he who "knows neither his right nor his left."

Chapter 30
A Psalm

What is a psalm? It is the song of a survivor, a poem that transforms one from a small person alone in the dark on a bed of misery, that describes enemies, and that calls out for help to the liberated man, the upright and confident man, who rejoices with and at the heart of the community. A psalm goes from supplication to praise, but there is never actually a response, which led the biblical scholar Paul Beauchamp to say that in a psalm, the silent response of God forms a scar, that of distress healed. At the end, in the praise, the community recognizes the salvation of the psalm's composer. The word "Hallelujah" means literally *louer Yah* (praise Yah) (the tetragram Yhwh). *The Book of Psalms* is a collection of different songs from various eras. The latest refer specifically to the historical conditions that followed the destruction of the Temple in 586 BCE. Others go back, no doubt, to the first generations of the dynasty of David (the tenth to ninth centuries BCE), which is why, in both the Jewish and Christian traditions, *The Book of Psalms* is attributed to the royal figure of David, who sang and played music to King Saul.

The one hundred and fifty psalms fall into different genres: psalms of supplication, of praise, of wisdom, messianic psalms, etc. But there's a poetic unity to them; the psalmist describes his distress, which is both intimate and historic, sometimes terrifying him almost to death. He wonders about Creation, its enigmas, its beauty, its dark parts. He observes the tragic absence of God but remembers past marvels of the patriarchs and of the Torah.

Chapter 31
Job

Job never existed; it's only a parable, says the Midrash. Every time there's a crisis in the history of the world that has been caused by human responsibility in the face of evil, the problem of Job comes up. "Our world is like old Job, overwhelmed and covered with sores on his pile of dung," claims Georges Bernanos in his *Journal of a Country Curate*. It's a world eaten away by the insupportable question of the arbitrary nature of misfortune and of its justification. The exiles in Babylon must also have remembered this story (an old Eastern legend) when they tried to understand their own unhappy situation. Ezekiel, the prophet of the exile, knew the story and counted Job among the Righteous. It's the terrifying story of a rich Arab (an Edomite, and therefore from an enemy nation), a model of wisdom, who lost everything simply because God made a bet with Satan, the Negater (from a verb that means "to deny, to oppose, to accuse"). Saint Augustine, in his *Confessions* (VII, 5, 7), states that the true subject of Job is the question of the origin of misfortune. Though Job lost everything, God did not take everything from him, said the Danish philosopher Søren Kierkegaard, with great insight. Job still had speech, which is to say, the ability to state his grievance and, above all, to contest his situation. Job represents all unhappy people who stand up and speak out to demand justice, to demand an accounting. Job testifies to a change in the representation of the God of Israel. The suffering man is struggling with God to the point of standing up to him—*that one might plead for a man with God*, to use the biblical expression (*The Book of Job*, 16:21). According to the Midrash, Job offers a poignant reinterpretation of the Torah. Suffering man is opposed to Creation, which he doesn't seem to recognize. The two monsters, Leviathan and Behemoth, represent the "nonhuman" of the Creation, in contradiction to the teachings of the Torah, in which man is the dominant creature (*The Book of Genesis* 1). It's as if these inhuman figures wipe out all temptation to anthropocentrism. For the anthropologist Mary Douglas, *The Book of Job* is an attempt to free all whom society has unjustly and brutally rejected from their feeling of having been cursed. "He who understands neither his condemnation nor his suffering carries the entire weight of the world," in the words of Simone Weil. Is that the reason that certain historians have gone as far as to imagine that the author of this book had seen a Greek tragedy?

Chapter 32
Esther

This story took place in the fifth century BCE in Shushan, the capital of the Persian empire, when it was at its height. A small Jewish community lived there in hiding. The Talmud asks: "Where do we get the idea that the *Book of Esther* is rooted in the Torah?" Esther is she who is in hiding, and where better to hide than in the Torah? God himself is hidden there. It is the only book in the Hebrew Bible in which God is not mentioned a single time. Esther lived with her adoptive uncle, Mordecai, and became the queen of a pagan people and history's first "Maranno" (one who practices Judaism in secret). The word "Maranno" comes from Jewish communities on the Iberian Peninsula in the fifteenth century who were converted to Catholicism, often by force, and yet continued to practice Judaism in secret. Rabbi Yehouda, in the Talmud, asks: "Her real name was Hadassah, so why the name of Esther? It's because she had hidden (*sater*) her true situation. Esther did not reveal her true origins." This gave rise to a fantastical etymology for the name, which Paul Claudel picked up on: "the hidden one." More accurately, her name is linked to the Persian goddess of night and of love, Astarta, or the Babylonian goddess of the moon, Ishtar. A "targum"—an annotated translation of the Hebraic or Aramaic Bible—states that she was as beautiful as "the evening star." She conquered the heart of the pagan king and married him. It's a strange fairy tale in which a little Jewish orphan in exile becomes a pagan queen and manages to thwart horror and extermination. The confrontation between the Jew Mordecai and the vizier Haman, a descendant of the Amalekite king Agag (saved by Saul and executed by Samuel), re-enacts the perpetual battle between Israel and its eternal enemy. What is at stake in this tale is the reversal of fate. They skirted catastrophe and celebrated an unbelievable escape. The one who ordered a massacre was himself massacred. *The Book of Esther* is the origin of the carnavalesque Jewish festival of Purim. While Passover celebrates the liberation of the Jewish people by great, visible miracles, Purim celebrates the invisible deliverance, deliverance by the hidden actions of God, and is named after the Assyrian word *purim*—the celebration of chance—because the date that Haman had planned for the massacre was drawn from a hat. The Talmud speaks of the "Purim games"—leaping over fires, solemn processions along which Haman is hanged or burned in effigy, a prohibition against drinking water, masquerades…

Chapter 33
Tobit

This small book was written to do good. It's another story of exile, and it dates from the first diaspora (722 BCE, the deportation from Judah to Assyria). Tobit, a pious and faithful Jew, was deported to Nineveh (the capital of Assyria, near what is today Mosul in Iraq). Having gone blind and in desperate straights, he sends his son to recoup some money lent to a relative now exiled in Ecbatana, in the Media region (now Iran). *The Book of Tobit* is a deuterocanonical text, i.e., one that is recognized by Christian churches but that is not included in the Hebrew Bible. Written in Hebrew or Aramaic, the original text was lost, but a copy was recovered in 1947 among the Dead Sea Scrolls. The book is, basically, a short novel about hope. Tobit, on the

one hand, reminds us of Job: faithful, pious, but desperately awaiting death. His young son, Tobias, undertakes a journey that is both an initiation and a training, and returns with his family's lost hope. Tobit also reminds us of Antigone, obsessed by his obligations to the dead. In the land of exile, the law prohibited the burial of fellow Jews according to the traditional rites. The debt to be recovered is symbolic. Tobias, the son, is sent to recover this debt, which has no other name but hope. On his route, Tobias must decide between love and death. It's a story of healing and salvation, and the Midrash evokes it as a kind of *haggadah* (ritual tale) of wisdom and hope—hope given to the young woman cursed by the demon Asmodeus, a Persian divinity of a misery and destruction, and hope and vision given back to the father and to the group of exiles. The name of the angel itself means "to heal" (*refa* in Hebrew); he is "the union of a body and an angel," at once a man, under the name of Azariah, and an angel, Raphael, according to the commentary of the medieval Franciscan philosopher and theologian William of Ockham (1285–1347). And finally, this small book condenses the active memory of the Torah by recalling the stories of Adam and Eve and of the Creation.

Chapter 34
Return from Exile

This story brings us two great biblical characters, two lives, but a single destiny consecrated to the return to Jerusalem and to the reconstruction. The two books of Ezra and Nehemiah speak (finally) of the return of the exiles and of their re-establishment in Judah at Jerusalem. The exiles first began returning in 538 BCE, the year that the Persian king Cyrus signed an edict allowing the deported Jews to return to their land, with the mission of rebuilding the Temple of Jerusalem, which had been destroyed by Nebuchadnezzar and the Babylonians. Isaiah went as far as giving Cyrus the title of messiah. But the royalty was not restored. The repatriated people had to learn to live under cultural and political domination and had to reconstruct their community— which didn't happen without difficulties. There was fighting because of mixed marriages and tensions between the diaspora and Judah, as well as between the indigenous and repatriated populations. The indigenous populations opposed the reconstruction of the wall that would mean their exclusion. It was Nehemiah, who had returned from Shushan and made several trips to Jerusalem, who was given the job of rebuilding the wall and its gates. The reconstruction of the Temple took twenty-three years. Ezra, the scribe, a specialist in the Scriptures of Moses, who had returned from Babylon, brought the Torah back to Israel, which, according to the Talmud, had forgotten it. The Torah was declared a sacred book, and was described as a second Moses. Its role was to remind the repatriated people of the Law of Moses and to gather together all the stories that they had remembered. The text of Ezra creates a parallel between the written Law and the rebuilt wall. The Law and the Book are also *gader*, a wall, an enclosure, protection (Ezra 9:9). Nehemiah summoned Ezra and asked him to read the Book (*sepher*) out loud before the standing people. The word *sepher* here takes on all its ritual and spiritual importance: *So they read in the book in the law of God distinctly, and gave the sense, and caused them to understand the reading* (Nehemiah 8:8).

Chapter 35
Daniel

Having returned from their exile, they once again had to confront the violence of History. *The Book of Daniel* inaugurates a new literary genre; inspired by ancient prophetic visions, its purpose is to offer an alternative understanding of time, an apocalyptic one (from a Greek word that means revelation, an uncovering). This literature appears with a conscious awareness of the dramatic nature of human history and the harsh effects of the Hellenization of the world, which included a crisis of various institutions (such as temple and royalty), the elimination of prophesy, and cultural and religious assimilation. *The Book of Daniel* proposes a new reading of History in order to revive past events and legends in a rather spectacular way while also underscoring the dramatic character of the present. Misery multiplied under the reign of King Antiochus IV

Epiphanes (175–164 BCE). Worship and sacrifices were forbidden in the Temple, which brought about a variety of troubles. Written in the Hellenistic period (333–63 BCE), while Palestine was under Seleucid rule and in light of contemporary events, *The Book of Daniel* reconsiders the time of the exile in grandiose fashion, with the legendary recollection of a young Hebrew hero, Daniel, who supposedly lived in Babylon in the sixth century BCE and was raised in the court of Nebuchadnezzar, where he performed miracles. It's understandable that the Talmud made Daniel into a hero of the resistance to assimilation in a foreign land, being that, at the time that it was written, the Judean community was divided on the question of Hellenistic domination. The story travels across epochs in order to enable a necessary understanding of violence and offer a way of healing the wounds of History through story, by recounting the difficulties of a traumatic past. For the biblical scholar Paul Beauchamp, here, the time of the end is not a "final" time, but instead is a time given to understanding and putting an end to wrong (*lekappêr 'awôn*: to put an end to transgression, *The Book of Daniel*, 9:24). Daniel is less a seer than a *maskil* (intelligent, educated). The *maskîlîm* read the Scriptures and interpreted them. Two major figures of this new understanding of time appear in this book: the "Son of man" (*The Book of Daniel* 7) and the first mention in the Bible of the resurrection of the dead. With the "Son of man," we abandon the traditional figures of the savior, the king, the chief, and the prophet in favor of an enigmatic expression that, in Hebrew and in Aramaic, means simply a man, someone. As for this first mention of the resurrection of the dead, "*And many of them that sleep in the dust of the Earth shall awake*" (*The Book of Daniel* 12:2), it is presented as "a condition absolutely essential to the universal application of the justice to come," according to the protestant theologian Jürgen Moltmann. It is a sign that there is an end to violence and evil. However, as the Talmud points out, we have been taught that man is nothing but dust and shall return to dust. But the great Pharisee Gamaliel in the first century would have replied by saying that God accomplishes the will of men who, through their hope and their thirst for justice, do not remain simply dust.

Table
of contents

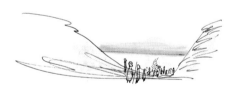

Library of Congress Cataloging-in-Publication Data available.

ISBN: 978-1-4521-6593-6

Manufactured in China.

Translation by Cole Swensen.
Art assistant contributions from Sheina Szlamka.

10 9 8 7 6 5 4 3 2 1

Chronicle Books LLC
680 Second Street
San Francisco, California 94107
www.chroniclebooks.com